Divorce and Second Marriage

DIVORCE AND SECOND MARRIAGE

Facing the Challenge

KEVIN T. KELLY

The Seabury Press · New York

1983
The Seabury Press
815 Second Avenue
New York, N.Y. 10017

Printed in the United States of America

Library of Congress Cataloging in Publication Data

Kelly, Kevin T., 1933-
    Divorce and second marriage.

    1. Divorce—Religious aspects—Catholic Church.
2. Remarriage—Religious aspects—Catholic Church.
3. Catholic Church—Doctrinal and controversial works.
I. Title.
BS2254.K44 1983   234'.165   83-680
ISBN 0-8164-2471-3 (pbk.)

CONTENTS

Contents

INTRODUCTION

Facing the challenge

Marriage breakdown and second marriage challenges all of us in the Church in a number of different ways.

It challenges us to put far more emphasis on proper preparation for marriage and on providing adequate support for married couples, especially during the critical phases of their marriage. It challenges us to be better equipped as a Church so that, wherever possible, we can help couples who are drifting apart to achieve a deep and lasting reconciliation. It challenges us, too, to offer deep understanding and support for men and women who have suffered the painful tragedy of their marriage breaking down completely, without any hope of reconciliation. Such people need support at a whole variety of levels to enable them to regain their balance and self-respect after such a devastating experience; and where there are children involved there are all the difficulties of one-parent families, with the additional problems of tension and rivalry between the separated parents and the consequent confusion and insecurity for the children. If such people choose to remain single as a sign of their commitment to life-long fidelity, the Church should feel challenged to give them every support possible.

These are all challenges which flow naturally from our belief in life-long marriage. However, vitally important though all these challenges are, they are not the ones which are faced in this book. Thank God, they are already being tackled more and more in the Church today and they have been very well high-lighted by the Pastoral Congress. This book would like to face a different set of challenges presented to us by second marriages after divorce. These are challenges which we find far more difficult to handle, since they do not fit in so easily with our belief in life-long marriage.

There is the challenge which increasingly many priests are experiencing, of the couple in such a second marriage who are

9

among the best parishioners in the community. Their home is a truly Christian home, their family is exemplary, they are fully participating members of the Eucharistic community and there is evident prayer and goodness in their lives. Priests are challenged by the obvious presence and activity of God's Spirit in the lives of these couples. Unless we are to separate off faith from life, and Vatican II considers this as one of the major errors of our day, there is no denying the Christian goodness of many second marriages of people who have been divorced. That is a challenge to us. How do we fit such marriages into our theology of marriage and our belief in the indissolubility of marriage? And how do we deal with such couples at the level of sacramental life?

Another challenge is one which faces almost all of us but which is felt most deeply by many parents. Someone close to us, perhaps a son or daughter, has gone through the tragedy of marriage breakdown and things have gone beyond the stage where reconciliation can realistically be hoped for. Has such a person no alternative but to remain single for the rest of life? Very often our concern for that person's deep happiness leads us to hope that he or she will find a new partner and will discover in a second marriage the happiness that eluded them in their first marriage. If our concern for that person's deep happiness is genuine, might it not be saying something to us about God's will? Can we be so certain that the life-giving Good News of Christ has no message except one of refusing healing when this is to be found in the love of a second marriage? That is a second challenge which we have to look at.

A further challenge is that of the millions of Catholic men and women now living in a second marriage after divorce. In the parish they may not be among the leading lights referred to above. There might not be anything particularly exemplary about their marriage and family life. But they are brothers and sisters to whom we believe the Gospel is addressed as Good News just as much as it is to the rest of us. The challenge we are faced with in their regard is this. Do we really believe that the Good News of Christ is calling them to break off and surrender the goodness of whatever married love now exists in their lives?

A personal note

This book is an attempt to face these last three challenges honestly. I have not found it an easy book to write, since by temperament I am cautious and very law-abiding, and at first sight this book might seem very brash and dismissive of authority. However, I have been impelled to write it by my conviction that these challenges come to us from the Lord himself. In them I feel he is beckoning us beyond our present certainties and securities. To refuse to face these challenges might be to refuse to listen to the Lord.

Although this book expresses my own personal and sincerely held views, it is the fruit of extensive reading and wide-ranging discussion over many years. My concern for the divorced-remarried was already aroused during the ten years in which I taught moral theology in the major seminary at Upholland. It was greatly consolidated by the very fruitful experience of sharing the problems of so many priests and lay-people while I was involved in Clergy In-Service Training and Adult Christian Education during my five years as Director of the Upholland Northern Institute. During that time I also served on the Working Party set up by the Bishops of England and Wales to look at the pastoral issues of the Sacrament to the Divorced-Remarried. And my brief experience in Skelmersdale New Town as leader of the Team Ministry there has only served to confirm me in my convictions. Consequently, if it does not sound too presumptious, I feel a certain peace and confidence in the position I am putting forward. I know that for the most part it is shared by the vast majority of my colleagues in the field of moral theology and that it is supported by the intuitive Christian sense of so many good priests and lay-people. But most of all I feel supported by the fact that what I have written seems to me to be in tune with what the Spirit is actually working out in the lives of so many people who are divorced and re-married, and in the courageous and welcoming ministry they are receiving from so many priests.

The argument of the book

I would summarise the main argument of this book as follows:
At Vatican II the Catholic Church reminded herself that she
must accommodate her understanding of the Gospel to the
richest insights and knowledge of every age and culture. This
does not mean watering down the truth. Nor is it just a matter
of mere translation into different and more appropriate language. It is a real challenge to the Church to listen to the
wisdom of her age. By so listening she will be able to penetrate
more deeply the truth she believes and so arrive at a fuller
understanding of it (cf. *The Church in the Modern World*, nn.44 &
58).

Despite the fact that there are many aberrations abroad today
about sexuality and marriage, it cannot be denied that there is
also a richer understanding of human sexuality and its relation
to growth in married love and parenthood. This deeper insight
has been gratefully received and acknowledged by Vatican II
and by Paul VI and John Paul II and has resulted in the
development of a much more satisfactory theology of marriage
as human reality and Sacrament.

There has been a dramatic change of gear in moving from
looking at marriage as a contract, to putting the main emphasis
on its being an inter-personal relationship of life-giving love.
These are not mutually exclusive positions, but one's whole
approach to marriage can alter radically depending on which is
made the main emphasis.

This change of gear fits in with the thesis proposed by
Thomas S. Kuhn in his famous work, *The Structure of Scientific
Revolutions* (University of Chicago Press, 1962). According to
Kuhn a particular science comes into being when some fertile
imagination discerns an overall pattern which brings together
and makes sense of what previously seemed to be a lot of
unconnected phenomena; and the science becomes established
when others working in the same field accept this overall
pattern and conduct all their research in accordance with it. The
consequent development of the science occurs through the
process of demonstrating how all sorts of other phenomena
also begin to make sense within that pattern. Kuhn calls such an

overall pattern a 'paradigm'. Phenomena which do not fit into the pattern are often discounted as being outside the field of this particular science, though there are usually some enterprising spirits who refuse to give up the challenge presented by these rogue phenomena. Kuhn maintains that a scientific revolution occurs when the adequacy of the accepted pattern is stretched to breaking point by the phenomena which cannot be accommodated within it, and the moment of breakthrough comes when another fertile imagination conceives a new pattern and suddenly things are seen to make sense in a new and different way. This initiates a new upsurge of scientific research as people explore all the exciting implications of viewing reality within this new pattern.

It seems to me that Kuhn's analysis can help us to understand what has occurred in the field of the theology of marriage. We are currently involved in the process of the change-over from one pattern to another. Society, with theology and the Church in its train, has moved from the 'contract' pattern of marriage to the 'relationship' pattern. Consequently, the present phase involves the exciting work of fitting all the pieces together again within this new pattern. For the Church this has wide implications for different levels of its life – law, pastoral policy, celebration of the sacraments, education etc. It is not surprising that many in the Church today complain of confusion during this phase. But it is not a confusion which is due to the Church having lost her way; it is merely a temporary, transitional confusion such as is necessarily involved in the process of changing position in order to get a better view of things. It is rather like the blurring of vision which occurs while one is trying to get things into clearer focus. In fact, it is a confusion which should eventually give way to a much clearer vision.

In this book I am trying to explore the implications of the 'relationship of life-giving love' pattern of marriage for a belief in the indissolubility of marriage. In no way do I wish to deny the indissolubility of marriage or to weaken it in any way. I want to see whether this new pattern of marriage allows us to see indissolubility in a new and richer light. If it does, I want to see what are the challenges this presents to us and whether it helps us to understand and interpret what is happening in our society, with its tragedy of such widespread breakdown of marriage. This is the main thrust of Chapters One and Two. I think it is only fair to state that the re-interpretation of indissolubility offered in these chapters does not carry the same wide consensus among moral theologians as the position and practice I put forward in Chapters Three and Four. This is not because many theologians have discussed it and rejected it. It is simply that it has not received wide discussion in theological journals; though I have a feeling that it should tie in with the general approach adopted by many of my colleagues. I look forward to their reactions, since I feel sure their comments should help to refine and tighten up the position I am proposing.

I also feel it is important to point out that Chapters Three and Four retain their validity independently of whether my re-interpretation of indissolubility is acceptable or not.

A listening Church

I am convinced that as a Church we need to be far more humble in our whole approach to marriage. We need to have the humility to listen to the experience of married people. This was a major strength of the National Pastoral Congress. It found such richness in the contribution of the married delegates that it recommended that the Church 'should listen to the experience of married people and appreciate their unique insights into what is contained within a permanent sexual relationship' (Sector C Report, n. 2). This recommendation was clearly listened to by the Bishops (cf. Easter People, n. 102) and Cardinal Hume made it his own in his first address to the 1980 Rome Synod on Marriage and the Family.

As a Church we also need the humility to listen to other cultures. In the 1980 Synod many Third World bishops expressed concern that a false conflict had been created between Gospel values and the values of their own particular cultures. They wanted the Church to be more attentive to the values of marriage and family as embodied in different cultures, since human and Christian values never exist in a non-cultural form. 'It could be left to the local Churches to embody this ideal in their different settings. It seems to be impossible to speak of a single model type of family valid for all people, cultures, and epochs. Each and every model is shaped by social and cultural circumstances' (Bishop Datubara of Indonesia). There is no pure state of marriage. Marriage is an institution which takes on different forms in different cultures.

Marriage in a cultural context

I am very much aware that I am writing this book in the specific cultural context of Western Christianity. Although human sexuality and its link with love and life transcends all cultures, it only exists in reality in particular cultural settings. That is why it is no disrespect to the fine teaching on marriage contained in the Vatican II Pastoral Constitution, *The Church in the Modern World* (nn. 47–52), to suggest that as a picture of the reality of marriage today it is probably a more accurate reflection of Western culture than of other cultures. This should be borne in mind later when I use such expressions as 'the Church's current understanding of the reality of marriage'. I can appreciate that some of the points I will be arguing in this book might lose much of their force in another cultural setting. This is particularly the case when we are looking at marriage as a relationship and trying to understand what happens when a marriage breaks down. I do not think that this invalidates my case. It simply means that to understand the indissolubility of marriage and its practical problems in parts of Africa or Asia, for instance, a different cultural view-point is needed. I respect the statement made to the Synod by Cardinal Rugambwa of Tanzania: 'The local Churches in Africa feel that they have the duty and the right to ensure that marriage and family life within their region are authentically Christian and authentically African. It is up to the local Churches to find solutions on the pastoral level to problems arising from Christianity and African cultures meeting each other'.

Origins of this book

These pages are by no means offered as a final solution. But neither are they merely a preliminary sketch. I have tried to blend together as well as I can the fruits of many people's reflection and practice in various parts of the Church, and I have added in some personal reflections of my own.

These pages were originally prepared as part of a joint work with Dr Jack Dominian. Circumstances beyond the control of both of us led to the abandonment of that venture. I am sure my debt to Dr Dominian still remains evident in what I have written and I have his written assurance that 'You have developed your theme of the internal relationship along lines that I would totally accept.' One sadness I have is that a book devoted entirely to looking at Divorce and Second Marriage might leave its author branded as one who betrays the Church's stand on life-long fidelity and the indissolubility of marriage. I hope I am as much committed to marriage for life as anyone. Although this book is not written jointly with Dr Dominian, I would be delighted if readers would see it as a kind of appendix to Dr Dominian's most recent work, *Marriage, Faith and Love* (DLT, 1981). That would guarantee that it was read in the context of an overall concern for married love in all its levels and in all its phases of development.

It would be impossible to mention by name all the people who through their sharing with me have played a part in helping this book to be written. However, I would like to thank especially my colleagues in the Association of Teachers of Moral Theology, with whom I have aired these concerns over many years; all my former associates in the Upholland Northern Institute both for their encouragement and for their practical help in making it possible for me to spend sabbatical leave on this book, and the Master and many friends at St Edmund's House, Cambridge, who were so kind to me during those months; and the members of the Skelmersdale Team Ministry who kept me going on the last lap when it was beginning to look as though the book might never be completed. I must also thank my fellow moral theologian and friend, Professor Charles Curran of the Catholic University of America, for his support and for his constructively critical observations on the original manuscript; and Frances Murphy for whom typing the final manuscript was far more than just a professional operation.

A final note by way of apology to my many women friends who have made me more conscious of sexist language. Due to the subject matter of this book I am constantly referring to one or other of the partners in a marriage. To use the 'he or she' idiom throughout the book would soon divorce me from the reader. Reluctantly I have accepted traditional usage and used 'he' in an indefinite sense. Does justice oblige me to use 'she' in the same way if I ever write another book on this subject?

Kevin T Kelly

Skelmersdale Team Ministry,
184, Liverpool Road,
Skelmersdale,
Lancashire.

1

A FRESH LOOK AT MARRIAGE AND INDISSOLUBILITY

COMING TO TERMS WITH MARRIAGE BREAKDOWN

Irreconcilable marriage breakdown is a human reality which the Catholic Church has to come to terms with in some way or other. Although many marriages with better preparation or support or with more adequate remedial care during the crisis periods might not have reached the state of irreconcilable breakdown, regrettably these helps were often not at hand when needed or at least were not made use of. Consequently, very many contemporary marriages which have broken down must be classified as 'irretrievable breakdowns'. In other words, whatever might be said about the future with its prospects of better educational, supportive and remedial care, for the present the Church has on her hands a crisis of marriage breakdown which cannot be solved by the mass reconciliation of divorced partners. The extent of this crisis is evident from the statistics for marriage breakdown in this country.

Apart from a small minority who see marriage as a purely temporary arrangement to be terminated at will, the majority of couples who marry do so in the hope that they will be able to share the rest of their lives together. That is what they think marriage and married love is all about. This means that none of them enter marriage with the intention of causing it to break down at a later date. Many will realize that such a breakdown is theoretically possible, though, like death, they will probably see it as something which happens to others. They do not really believe it could happen to *their* marriage. Therefore, if both of them genuinely intend to marry for life, something quite different to what they intend must happen between them if the situation becomes changed so drastically that they reach the stage of irreconcilable breakdown.

In *Marriage, Faith and Love*, Dr Dominian has described the typical stages of growth or crisis through which most marriages have to pass. The passage through these stages does not happen automatically. All these stages can be painful and in some cases couples may not have the inner resources necessary to make the transition. Sometimes too the external pressures might be too great for them. This might be expressed slightly differently by saying that many couples may not understand what is happening to them when they reach the troubled waters of these stages and they may be thrown badly off course without realizing what is going on. Furthermore, until recently society in general had little appreciation of the different stages involved in the process of development within marriage. And so, much of the external help which was offered to the couple might have been quite unsuitable to their needs.

Consequently, it would seem fair to say that frequently the cooling off of fidelity in marriage is not a positive choice made by one partner or the other. The couple suddenly find it is happening; but why it is happening is a mystery to them. Like any other symptom, its only real cure lies in tackling its root cause but this root cause is not understood by those immediately affected. So the symptom itself is treated since it is thought to be the actual cause. This only leads to disaster in one form or another. The inner love of the marriage continues to disintegrate and the marriage dies. The couple separate or else they settle down to living what is no more than an empty shell of a marriage.

Is the sin of one or both partners the real cause of marriage breakdown? In most cases probably not, I would suggest, since, as already noted, couples normally enter marriage with every intention of staying together and the death of their marriage is the very last thing they want. That might be true, one could object, but their good intentions can easily evaporate when they meet some of the difficulties involved in married life and it is this hardly perceptible transition from good to bad will which causes their marriage to come asunder.

But does this really correspond to people's experience? Many couples who have been through this traumatic experience would claim that their marriage broke down despite their genuine efforts to save it. It is true that they eventually chose to separate but probably at that stage everyone agreed that such a decision was the only reasonable choice open to them. So it could hardly be described as a sinful decision.

But what about during the actual process of breakdown? Was there not clear evidence of bad will in all the hurt they inflicted on each other or in the way they withdrew their love in various ways? In many instances, these injuries to each other could probably be described as 'sins of passion'. In other words, they did not come out of an evil heart but resulted from an inability to cope with an emotional reaction to a situation which seemed beyond their control and outside their normal experience. 'What on earth is happening to us?' are not just words spoken on the stage; they belong very much to the real-life drama of marriage breakdown.

Is this interpretation fatalistic? Is it suggesting that couples can do nothing to stop their marriage breaking down and that they bear no responsibility for the breakdown? Not at all. This view would in fact be saying that they and they alone are the only ones who are able to make their marriage and that therefore only they can prevent its breakdown. Thank God, more succeed in this than fail. That is why marriage breakdown is still the exception rather than the rule. Surely to say that is a far cry from fatalism! But this view is also suggesting that, although only the couple themselves can make their marriage, nevertheless the reason why so many fail in this need not be their own bad will, but may often be their lack of understanding of what is going on and their consequent inability to cope. However, I am not denying that it can sometimes happen that a marriage can be destroyed through the serious and persistent fault of one of the partners. Nevertheless, I would hazard the generalization that in Western society today the basic attitude of ordinary men and women towards marriage is fundamentally good. More specifically, Vatican II's vision of the human reality of marriage as a covenant of interpersonal love which is faithful and life-giving would seem to correspond to the deepest desires and convictions of most men and women, inside and outside the Church.

If this is an accurate picture, why is there such a vast increase in marriage breakdown? Dr Dominian suggests that this is because of the heightened expectations which men and women bring to marriage. Obviously, these flow from the contemporary view of sexuality and marriage. A few of these expectations (e.g. judging sexual adequacy by false standards of maximum performance) might be quite unreal and artificially cultivated by advertising and the media. Nevertheless, generally speaking most of the expectations can be accepted as good and appropriate, arising as they do from a positive attitude to sexuality and marriage. This means, therefore, that in entering marriage today a couple are making a greater investment in their personal relationship than was ever done in the past. This is very healthy because the human reality of marriage at the present day is such that unless the personal relationship is firmly based there is little hope that the marriage will survive, at least in a form that would be regarded as desirable. It is not realistic to say that contemporary expectations of marriage are too high and that if couples would only lower their sights they would have no problem with their marriage. These expectations do not concern some incidental benefits which they hope to draw from their marriage. They touch the very heart of what the couple believe their marriage to be. Consequently, if these expectations are not fulfilled, their marriage is experienced by them as something which does not make sense, as something which is self-contradicting and a lie. That is why they feel it would destroy them as persons if they were to continue with it. Men and women cannot continue to invest their persons in something which they experience as person-destroying.

The fact that so many marriages today end in breakdown forces us to look again at our belief in the indissolubility of marriage. An outside observer looking at society today would see plenty of empirical evidence for believing that marriage is not indissoluble. Tragically, marriage seems to be far too dissoluble. So can we as Christians still maintain a realistic belief in the indissolubility of marriage? I believe we can and we must. But this belief must be in tune with the reality of marriage as it is experienced and lived today.

THE REALITY OF MARRIAGE TODAY

The human reality of marriage in Western culture today differs in some important respects from marriage in previous ages and even in some contemporary cultures. Some of these differences touch the very heart of what marriage is understood to mean. For instance, while it is possible to recognize that St Augustine and the Fathers of Vatican II are speaking about the same basic reality when they discuss marriage, it is also true to say that in at least one essential aspect they understand it differently. St Augustine could never have written section 49 of Vatican II's *The Church in the Modern World*, which goes to the heart of how the Church interprets the goodness of married love today. For him it would have been unthinkable to have suggested that sexual intercourse between a married couple could be the vehicle by which their love 'merging the human with the divine . . . is uniquely expressed and perfected'. While St Augustine in some parts of his writings allows for the possibility of a real friendship between husband and wife (even though some of his other remarks are hard to reconcile with this), nowhere does he come near to suggesting that this friendship could be mediated through sexual intercourse.

Today great emphasis is put on the personal relationship which constitutes a marriage and the sexual dimension of this relationship is better appreciated. This is very much in evidence in the current approach to marriage preparation. It concentrates on helping an engaged couple to look at the quality of their relationship so that they can build on its strengths and rectify or at least be aware of its weaknesses. Likewise, as was clearly acknowledged by the Pastoral Congress (Sector C, Topic 2), any sound pastoral policy of support within marriage will try to help couples to move constructively through the various critical phases of their relationship and it will offer the appropriate help needed at each stage. All this is based on a firm belief that it is the human reality of the couple's relationship which forms the heart of their marriage. To use other terms, the matter of the sacrament of marriage is the human relationship of the couple themselves.

This is not ignoring the social dimension of marriage. Marriage is a fundamental social institution and in all societies it is very wisely enhanced and protected by a whole variety of laws, customs and rituals. It is from this angle that down through the ages the Church has concentrated on marriage as a solemn contract. Understandably, this has been the aspect emphasised in Canon Law. Regrettably, until very recently it has also been the viewpoint of most moral theologians over the past few centuries, often due to an amalgamation of the teaching roles of moral theologian and canon lawyer.

Today the Church denies neither the social dimension of marriage nor its character as a contract; but it does insist that the heart of marriage lies in its being an inter-personal sexual relationship of life-giving love, and one which is therefore permanent and exclusive. It is this relationship which is given the legal status of a contract and institutionalized in various other ways; but it is neither the contractual character nor the institutional factors which tell us about the reality of marriage. For that we have to go to the relationship. It is there that we find the most basic and fundamental reality of marriage.

This is the clear teaching of the Fathers of Vatican II in their Pastoral Constitution, *The Church in the Modern World* (nn. 47–52). It was warmly embraced by Paul VI and finds eloquent expression in his encyclical, *Humanae Vitae*, (epsecially nn. 8–9). In fact, the reason why so many theologians and lay-people found certain sections of that encyclical so unacceptable was not simply because they did not like what he said, but because it seemed in contradiction to this basic understanding of marriage as a relationship of life-giving love. The disputed passage seemed inconsistent with the rich vision of the earlier part of the encyclical and out of tune with the mind of Vatican II.

This same personalist approach to marriage is also the stance of Pope John Paul II and is spelled out at length in his recent Apostolic Exhortation, *Familiaris Consortio*, in which he tries to share with the rest of the Church the fruits of the 1980 Synod on Marriage and the Family. Here too there are some practical points with which very many theologians and married people would disagree, but at least the debate can be carried on within a mutually acceptable vision of marriage as a personal relationship of life-giving love.

To say that marriage is for life can make it sound like a life-sentence. The Church's current understanding of marriage is really saying that it is for life (i.e. life-long) because married love is all about giving life and that is a life-long process. This brings out the intimate connection between the couple's love for each other and the fruitfulness of that love, usually resulting in giving life to their children. In speaking of marriage as a personal relationship the Church insists that married love must be 'open to life' or 'life-giving'. I prefer to use the latter express-ion; its full meaning is appreciated only when the intimate unity between both aspects of married love is understood.

In the first place their love is life-giving to each other. Husband and wife through their mutual love and trust enable each other to become alive in ways they never believed possible. They may be able to heal some of the personal handicaps each brings into the marriage from negative experiences in earlier life. They support each other and are able to help each other grow as individuals and in the process they grow as a couple. Since what is being talked about is not just physical life but the developing life of persons, it is not just romantic imagery to describe the couple's love as being in the first instance life-giving for themselves.

Their love is also life-giving in the sense of giving life to new persons, their children. While it is possible to read too much significance into physical processes, most Christians would be prepared to see the hand of God in the fact that the very act by which a couple is said to 'make love' to each other includes within it the power to give life to a new person. Naturally, the moment of conception or birth is not seen as the end of this second way in which their love is life-giving. They are giving life not just to a living human organism but to a *person*. The 1980 Synod put this very simply: 'The end product of procreation is the person and he is only fully brought alive when he is properly educated' (Proposition 26, no. 2). In other words, the life-giving power of a couple's love is at work all through the process of the upbringing and education of their children. They are bringing their children alive as loving persons. Once again this is not just mere imagery. Psychologists never tire of insisting that one of the most influential factors in the personal development of a child is the climate of love, acceptance and security found in a home where parents have a genuine love for each other. If a couple's love is not truly life-giving to each other, it will not be able to be fully life-giving to their children either. Without the secure home background of their parents closely united together, it is more difficult for the children to become more fully alive and develop as persons capable of forming loving relationships. Furthermore, it is probably true to say that normally the growth of the parents' love for each other needs the stimulus of their shared love for their children. In other words, there is a very real sense in which children can actually give life to their parents; they can bring them more fully alive. The wheel of life-giving love turns a full circle.

The Church's current understanding of marriage sees all these facets of life-giving love as intimately bound together. Sadly, at the level of official teaching she has still not been able to draw out the full implications of this as regards life-giving love and family planning. In an Appendix to this book I have included my own attempt to spell out these implications.

There is a richness in the contemporary understanding of marriage that is not to be found in earlier ages. This is something at which a Christian must rejoice, since he interprets this deeper understanding as a fuller appreciation of God's truth. Nor is this just at the level of ideas. It has obvious implications for the way people can actually live their marriages. Marriage today offers a much richer personal life than was ever thought possible in times past.

There is no doubt that marriage is for life; that is, it is about giving and sharing life with other persons. There is also no doubt that the Church has always taught that marriage is for life in the sense of being permanent, life-long.

In no way do I want to deny or even challenge that teaching. What I want to do is to see whether the Church's contemporary emphasis on marriage as a personal relationship of life-giving love helps to throw any new light on the way we understand the permanence or indissolubility of marriage.

INDISSOLUBILITY, A TASK FOR LIFE

Indissolubility and the personalist approach to marriage
In earlier ages the fact that marriages were able to last for life was partly due to the many external supports and constraints which helped to hold them together. This is not to suggest that in many instances there was not a deep personal love between the couple. When that was there, a marriage would have an inner permanence of a very different nature to that of many other marriages which would be kept in being almost entirely by these external factors.

Furthermore, the permanence or indissolubility of marriage was not clearly seen as flowing from the nature of the couple's love for each other. That is why their interpersonal love was not thought to be essential to their marriage and its indissolubility. The main point of focus was the institutional character of marriage. The emphasis was put on the solemn contract to which the couple gave their consent. The contract spelled out what marriage was all about, with each partner's rights and duties. Marriage was seen more as an institution which they entered, rather than as an interpersonal reality which they themselves brought into existence. Indissolubility was considered to be one of the essential properties of marriage, rather than something flowing from the very nature of the couple's love for each other. While there was a deep appreciation of its importance for the good of the children and the stability of the family and society, its ultimate binding force was traced back to the command of God 'in the beginning', reiterated by Christ himself.

As already stated, the Church today does not deny that marriage is an institution. It is obviously a crucial element in the fabric of society. But it is not the needs of society which determine what marriage should be. In fact, the very reason why marriage is an important institution within society is precisely because of its nature as an interpersonal reality of life-giving love. That is why the roots of the indissolubility of marriage must not be sought in the good of society but in the very nature of the committed life-giving love of a couple for each other. It can be spoken of as being 'commanded' by God only because it is in fact demanded by our being truly human. And it is in the experience of this truly human fidelity that we get some inkling of and feel for (and even involvement in) the fidelity of God himself.

It would seem that the personalist approach to marriage can give us a renewed and richer understanding of indissolubility. Indissolubility is something which has to be brought into being *within the marriage itself*. When they marry, a couple do not suddenly find themselves tied by an indissoluble bond which has an existence independent of them. When they marry, they give their pledge that they will form an indissoluble union of persons through their love for each other. The indissolubility of their marriage is *a task to be undertaken*.

A closer look at indissolubility

This proposition needs closer analysis. It is not saying that it is up to the couple to decide whether they want a soluble or an indissoluble marriage. Obviously, they are free to choose the former if they so wish, but in that case I would say that what they have chosen is not marriage in the true sense. It is not so much that they are rejecting one of the essential properties of marriage. It is more that they are pledging themselves to married love while refusing that commitment of unconditional trust to each other which is the indispensable first step needed to bring married love into existence.

Indissolubility is in no way an optional extra open to the free choice of the couple. It flows from the very nature of the love they are pledging to each other. This is clearly stated by Vatican II: 'As a mutual gift of two persons, this intimate union, as well as the good of the children, imposes total fidelity on the spouses and argues for an unbreakable oneness between them' (*The Church in the Modern World*, n. 48). This text is taken up and reaffirmed by Pope John Paul II in his Apostolic Exhortation, *Familiaris Consortio*, n. 20. It is beyond the scope of this book to attempt to prove that life-long fidelity is an essential quality of married love. I would suggest that, as well as being taught by Vatican II, recent Popes and the Synod, this view is accepted by all Christians and Christian Churches today. It would also seem to be the prevailing view in society at large, at least in Western culture. It is not contradicted by the fact that there is a widespread breakdown of marriage. On the contrary, the fact helps to prove it. Men and women want a marriage based on interpersonal love and they are refusing to be bound by an indissolubility which they feel has no foundation in interpersonal love. Consequently, they believe that when love in marriage has completely died indissolubility has lost its roots.

This indissolubility is not something independent of the couple of themselves. Their children, other people, the Church and society may expect it from them but its reality lies in themselves. That is why I would prefer to speak of the life-long fidelity of married love rather than of the indissolubility of marriage. I recognize that the latter term is firmly enshrined in traditional usage. Nevertheless, it seems more in keeping with the contemporary understanding of marriage to view its permanence or indissolubility as a consequence of the life-long fidelity of married love. In other words, it is the faithfulness of married love which is really fundamental. It is towards this that the Church should be directing its attention.

I am claiming not only that fidelity is an essential quality of married love, but also that it is a quality which can grow and develop only along with the growth and development of married love itself. Therefore, to understand this fidelity the nature of married love itself needs to be looked at.

It takes two to make love – and to make indissolubility
A catch-phrase common in Marriage Encounter circles today is: *love is a decision*. Since fidelity is a quality of married love, it could also be said that fidelity too is a decision. The meaning

behind the catch-phrase is that the decision to love is not taken once and for all and then everything else follows automatically. Love is only real as a decision to the extent that it is continually renewed in big and small matters throughout the course of married life.

The important thing to notice is that it takes two to make love. Consequently, it takes two to make the decision to love. When one partner begins to refuse to renew the decision in the events of their life together, the other is forced into the position of trying single-handed to keep their love alive. This would involve a decision to work at healing, reconciliation, forgiveness etc. If these are continually refused, it becomes impossible to make their love last. Obviously, this will all depend on whether the situation can be mended or not. As long as reconciliation is believed to be a real possibility, fidelity as a decision still retains a true meaning in the context of this marriage. There are definite actions which can be undertaken which are a realistic way of giving practical effect to the decision to be faithful in love. They are realistic because they have a genuine connection with the hoped-for reconciliation. The decision not to re-marry is an obvious example.

However, if the situation is so far gone that there is absolutely no possibility of reconciliation, the picture changes completely. In this case, love no longer exists, because the joint decision on which it depends for its very existence has ceased to operate. Of course, one of the partners, the husband for instance, might still feel he is in love with his wife. Since he considers that he has not refused the decision to love, he might decide to remain faithful to his initial decision. At one level this might be admirable; at another level it could be tragic. He feels he is being faithful to his marriage. I would suggest that perhaps it no longer exists for him to be faithful to. This is not to suggest that his 'fidelity' is without value. Human tragedy can at times be a most powerful witness to the ideals which have occasioned it. Pope John Paul II has a special word of praise for men and women who give such a witness (*Familiaris Consortio*, n. 20).

Irreconcilable breakdown – a denial of God's love?

The Bible often portrays God as the faithful husband who is always ready to forgive his erring wife no matter how unfaithful she may have been. Since marriage is a symbol of this faithful love of God, is not the notion of irreconcilable breakdown a denial of this symbolism? Does the admission that reconciliation is impossible deny the power of God's reconciling love?

This is a serious theological objection and deserves careful attention. Perhaps the following remarks could be made with reference to it.

Married love is a symbol of God's love. However, it cannot be completely identified with God's love. Somehow Catholic theology has manoeuvred itself into the position of holding that whatever can be said of God's love applies without further qualification to the love of every married couple. This is not true. By overloading the meaning of symbol in this area, Catholic theology can be doing married couples a disservice. It can change the privilege of being a symbol of God's love into an intolerable burden for some married couples. The *true* symbolism of marriage is encouraging for a couple, since it invites them to let their human love grow more and more into the likeness of God's own love. To totally identify their love with God's love can dehumanize their love and can leave them confused and disheartened by the contrast they see between their own human imperfect love, with all its limitations and imperfections, and the perfection of God's love.

Therefore, to accept that human married love can break down irretrievably does not imply that the same is true of God's love. Despite the mysterious words of Jesus about the unforgivable sin, it is part of Christian faith to believe that no one can be so far gone in sin as to be completely beyond the reach of God's forgiving love. In other words, irretrievable breakdown is an unthinkable notion when applied to God's love for his people. Presumably this is because at the very centre of every human person lies some kind of innate desire for God. This cannot be extinguished without a person's very humanity ceasing to exist. So the reason why the total and irretrievable breakdown between God and mankind is inconceivable is not just because of the nature of God's love as it exists in himself; it is also because of the corresponding desire for his love which he has placed in every man and woman.

This is not true of the love of a particular man and woman for each other. Though there is a beautiful saying, 'Marriages are made in heaven', it is no part of Christian faith to believe that married couples are destined for each other by God. Certainly, what draws them together is far more than a rational decision to love. Every marriage carries its own personal story of what attracts the partners to each other. Usually there will be factors working on all the five levels outlined by Dr Dominian – social, sexual, emotional, intellectual and spiritual (*Marriage, Faith and Love* DLT, 1981 Part III). These factors have a vital part to play in attracting the partners to each other and in helping them to grow closer together and to develop and mature in their two-in-oneness. The general way in which this process works is clearly described by Dr Dominian. From that analysis it is quite obvious that far more needs to be said than that love is a decision. For love to develop and grow there needs to be some kind of awareness of what is going on at these various levels. Commitment (a better word than decision) is not enough. Without this awareness the various factors which have worked to draw the partners together can begin to have the opposite effect and drive them apart again. Or in some instances perhaps some of the factors which should have been working if the couple were to draw really close together, might not have been operative; and then suddenly they might begin to make their presence felt but only with the effect of showing the couple how far apart they are from each other.

Therefore, although there may be some truth in the saying 'Love is a decision', it is at least equally true to say that married love consists in a number of clearly identifiable components. Each of these needs to be operating at least at a minimum level if married love is to grow properly and mature. When some of the more important components are absent or are ignored or even violated, married love will only be present in a seriously defective form and there is a real danger that it will deteriorate and die. A renewed decision to love will not be enough to stop this happening. The precise factors which are causing the trouble will need to be tackled if there is to be any hope of recovery. However, some of these factors might be outside the control of the couple. For example, despite their willingness to give it another chance, a couple's marriage might still break up simply because they are quite incompatible either sexually or personality-wise. It is possible that a marriage might die, not because the couple were not committed to life-long fidelity, but because they did not know how to love each other. They never lost their belief in life-long fidelity, but the source of their fidelity to each other dried up because they were unable to cope with the process of growing in married love.

Married love has its own very specific needs, therefore. That is why, although it may be a symbol of God's love, it is unhelpful and even misleading to suggest that what can be said of God's love can be applied without qualification to married love.

Does interpreting indissolubility in the way I have suggested mean that I am rejecting the whole tradition of the Church in the West? Far from it. There are various elements in the Latin Church's traditional practice which would offer some support for the position I have outlined.

Some lessons from history

The Catholic Church's current teaching and practice with regard to indissolubility has undergone considerable development throughout history. What most interests us here is the way the Church has gradually evolved a position which recognizes different degrees of indissolubility. In other words, while she believes in the indissolubility of marriage, she also accepts that most kinds of marriage can be dissolved. In fact, the only kind of marriage which she holds to be absolutely indissoluble is a valid marriage between baptized persons which has been consummated. She accepts the possibility of the dissolution of every other kind of marriage. How did this come about? After all, it seems a strange development in view of the fact that the teaching of Jesus is so clear: marriage breakdown, divorce and remarriage are not God's plan for men and women. Moreover, Jesus is not giving this as teaching which applies only to his own followers. 'It was not so from the beginning'. In other words, marriage breakdown, divorce and remarriage contradict the very nature of marriage itself. In God's design every marriage is called to life-long fidelity.

Paul took the first important step. He found that the marriages of some of his converts still broke down despite the radical teaching of Jesus. In fact, some broke down precisely because one of the partners became a Christian. To ease the situation Paul told them that if they were not able to live at peace with their non-Christian partners they were no longer bound. Paul's pastoral ruling was later developed still further by the Church: such a Christian could remarry another Christian and in such a case it was recognized that the former marriage had ceased to exist. This is known as the Pauline Privilege and still operates in the Church today.

Moreover, in what has been called the 'Petrine Privilege' which in our century went through some dramatic developments under Pius XII, the Church extended even further the implications of Paul's ruling that one should be able to live at peace as a Christian. The Church will dissolve the marriage of two non-Christians if it can be shown that such a dissolution will help a Christian third party to live at peace in marriage. This same broad-minded pastoral approach was adopted by a series of Popes in the handling of the marriage problems of captives and slaves in the sixteenth century and their decisions still have a place in current Church law. Implied in all these practices of the Church would seem to be the assumption that not being able to sustain their marriage relationship in peace is an essential element in the Church's determining that there is no longer any marriage in these instances.

Another important step was the compromise solution adopted by Pope Alexander III in the dispute between Paris and Bologna as to whether it was consent or consummation which made a marriage. He accommodated both views by ruling that it was consent which made the marriage but it was consummation which finally gave it absolute indissolubility. In practice this meant that Alexander was recognizing two degrees of indissolubilty even in marriages between two Catholics. This is relevant for our discussion of indissolubility since it shows that the Church did not look on marriage as absolutely indissoluble simply because it was a sacrament. Over the years the Church's practice became established: a non-consummated sacramental marriage could be dissolved either by a decision of the Pope or by the relationship ceasing to be effective through one partner taking solemn religious vows.

Indissolubility: its strength and its fragility

Since the above paragraphs have looked at the way in which marriages, called to be indissoluble in the design of God, can actually dissolve, it might help to say more precisely what is meant by the indissolubility of marriage. In this chapter I have been arguing that at least in Western society today the indissolubility of marriage depends on the continued growth and development of the couple's love for each other. This is where its great strength lies, even though it is also the source of its fragility. This is really saying that indissolubility is something to be realized in a marriage. A man and a woman getting married bind themselves by a solemn commitment to love each other faithfully for the rest of their lives. Indissolubility is the fruit of this pledged life-long love. The process of building their love together depends on commitment, trust and understanding from within and an appropriate and timely support from without. It is in the very process of building this love that they create the indissolubility of their marriage. One would be missing the point to argue that this really means that a marriage is only indissoluble when it has actually lasted until one partner has died. That is true if 'indissoluble' is being used in a purely descriptive sense. But Christians believe it has a deeper meaning than that, it refers to the deeper levels of personal being. The initial foundation of the indissolubility of marriage lies in the fidelity of these two persons to their committed word and the trust they invest in each other. That is already a deep basis in their being as persons. They have made solemn marriage vows to God and to each other and they have made an act of faith that each will be faithful to those marriage vows. This in itself is a very substantial foundation for the initial indissolubility of their marriage. An unconditional commitment to life-long fidelity is a personal act of the greatest significance. But it is a commitment to undertake and achieve something. It is not the achievement itself. Personal fidelity to one's committed word is a most sacred obligation, but it can be thwarted. However, as they grow together and become 'two in one flesh' in the sense already explained, the indissolubility of their marriage gains an even deeper basis. It is now founded on the oneness they have achieved as a couple. In a sense, they are now a new being, not just 'I' and 'you' but also 'we'. The Church of England report, *Marriage and the Church's Task*, has expressed this beautifully:

> The marriage bond unites two flesh-blood-and-spirit persons. It makes them the persons that they are. It binds them together, not in any casual or peripheral fashion, but at the very centre of their being. They become the persons they are through their relationship to each other. Each might say to the other 'I am I and I am you; together you and I are we'. Since the marriage bond is in this way a bond of personal *being*, it is appropriate to speak of it as having an 'ontological' character (section 96).

I do not think that the position I have been outlining is a denial of indissolubility. It is merely a different way of understanding it. Admittedly, it accepts the possibility that some marriages (far too many at present) will not attain this inner indissolubility and instead will disintegrate and fall apart so that eventually they no longer exist. This is not to deny that these marriages were never indissoluble in any sense. They were; but their indissolubility during that initial stage drew its binding force from the pledged commitment they had made to each other to become two-in-one at a deep personal level. It was not yet based on the achievement of that personal two-in-oneness. Sadly these marriages never reached that level of indissolubility. To understand indissolubility as having two levels of binding force should not seem too outrageous to Roman Catholics brought up on the earlier way of viewing marriage. As had been noted already, it is only possible to make sense of some aspects of the Latin Church's practice by admitting that some marriages are more indissoluble than others.

No to conditional marriage vows?

It might be objected that my understanding of indissolubility would mean that the commitment given in the marriage vows would in reality only be conditional and so it would be more honest to add in some qualifying clause such as 'for as long as our relationship lasts'. That does not follow at all. The couple's commitment is to life-long fidelity and that is precisely why they are morally obliged to do all in their power to achieve that fidelity. By moral obligation here I mean that their personal integrity is at stake, they have committed themselves to this task. To insert a qualifying clause into their commitment would completely alter the nature of the commitment they are making to each other. It would mean that the breakdown of their marriage could not be described as evil since it would be quite in accord with the pledge they had given each other.

The approach I have been describing is quite different. It sees two distinct but not unrelated elements in the commitment the couple make. One is the obligation by which each is bound by virtue of his or her commitment. This is the obligation to fulfil the task to which they have committed themselves. The other element is the task itself to which they are committed. This is to fuse their lives together into an unbreakable personal union. To admit the possibility that some couples might fail (culpably or unculpably) in the task in no way implies that the original commitment should only be conditional. In fact, from the very nature of the task being undertaken the commitment needs to be unconditional.

2

CAN A CHRISTIAN CHOOSE A SECOND MARRIAGE AFTER DIVORCE?

In the Roman Catholic Church the answer to that question has been a qualified 'Yes'.

A second marriage after divorce is acceptable if the first marriage is not considered to have been a true marriage in the proper sense of the word (null or invalid); or if the first marriage is considered to be no longer binding (Pauline Privilege or Papal Dissolution).

This chapter looks more closely at these possibilities and examines whether any new light is thrown upon them by the change of emphasis in the theology of marriage. Does the shift of emphasis from contract to relationship alter their focus at all and, if so, what implications has this for the way we look at second marriages today? But before we undertake this analysis it might be appropriate to remind ourselves that we are not trying to solve some kind of pastoral puzzle; we are thinking about the lives of people who have been deeply wounded through suffering the human tragedy of marriage breakdown.

THE HUMAN TRAGEDY OF MARRIAGE BREAKDOWN

Marriage breakdown is a human tragedy. It causes hurt and suffering to human persons. It can crucify a husband and wife and their children, as well as family and friends. In the home and relationship where they are hoping for mutual healing and support and where they are expecting that atmosphere of trust and security needed for them to grow further as human persons, they eventually find the very opposite – mistrust, insecurity and even hatred. We put things the wrong way round if we assert that divorce is evil because it is forbidden by God. That does not face the question: why is divorce against God's will? The answer to that question is found in a statement of St Thomas Aquinas which could be paraphrased as: God is not offended by us except insofar as we harm ourselves and other people. Marriage breakdown and divorce is evil because of the human hurt and suffering caused by it. It offends God because people precious to him are being harmed and are hurting each other. That is why it is a human tragedy.

Marriage breakdown is a form of dying. For most people it entails an experience of deep pain. Especially for the partners in the marriage there is a crushing sense of rejection and personal failure. There is the guilt of feeling that they have failed God, themselves and their family and friends. This can wreak havoc with their sense of self-worth.

Any major dislocation of a person's life puts him under severe personal strain. Marriage breakdown is an experience which involves serious disruption of life at many levels. Emotionally a person is affected very deeply. Often a person becomes so drained at this level that the emotions have to be drawn out of the marriage even before the initial separation. The economic disruption can be painful particularly for the wife. At a legal level a person can be shattered by the frightening and dehumanizing character of the court procedure, especially when the question of custody of the children and access to them comes before the court. On the social level, the normal pattern of relationships is now broken since much of social intercourse is based on the unit of the couple. A divorced person can be a source of embarrassment to his or her friends. Psychologically a husband or wife has to readjust to the challenge of living alone. As regards the children, they have to get used to the change from a two-parent to a one-parent family as well as the confusion and emotional blackmail they can experience when one of the parents uses them as a pawn against the other.

Many people who have been through the experience of marriage breakdown liken it to the experience of bereavement. There can be similar patterns of behaviour to the grief process – disbelief and denial that this is happening; anger at the unfairness of it; bargaining to put something in its place; depression and final acceptance. Men and women who have been through the tragedy of marriage breakdown are wounded people. They need appropriate care. Most certainly this care does not consist in condemnation or rejection by the community. Nor does it involve encouraging them to bounce on the rebound into a hasty second marriage. In fact, such an unwise second marriage can actually be caused by rejection or condemnation on the part of the community. The appropriate care they need is to be brought back to life again so that they can make a new beginning.

The thrust of our pastoral care must always be one of healing. Sometimes that healing will take the form of reconciliation between the couple and they are helped to rebuild their disrupted life. But sometimes that form of healing is no longer possible. Perhaps the true foundations of a lasting marriage were not there in the first place. Maybe the wounds go too deep and are beyond repair. It might be that one partner or other has formed a new and permanent relationship and there is no going back on this.

In such a situation healing has to take another form. If the community is sensitive to the needs of someone who has been through the painful experience of marriage breakdown, that healing might take place in the context of a positive acceptance of not remarrying as long as such a decision did not flow from a fear of risking a new relationship. Sadly, however, it can happen that some communities are not alert to the needs of such people. What then? In some instances the only setting in which effective healing might be found might be in a second marriage. Experience seems to show that this can and does happen. When it does happen, it must surely be God's healing touch which is being experienced since all genuine human healing comes ultimately from him. Someone who was lost has now found himself. The Christian is called to rejoice at this, rather than resent it after the manner of the elder brother.

It is only in this context of the Church celebrating the healing action of God in our lives that any discussion of the possibility of second marriage after divorce has any chance of getting a proper hearing among Christians. The fact that Catholics are becoming more conscious of this healing at work in the second marriages of their friends and even their relatives is making them more open to look at the underlying question as to whether a second marriage after divorce is a choice which is open to a Christian.

NULLITY AND THE 'RELATIONSHIP' APPROACH TO MARRIAGE

To say that a marriage is null is to say that it has never been a real marriage right from the beginning. This is a different notion to that of divorce, which involves saying that a real marriage has now ceased to be or at least is no longer legally binding.

The concept of nullity did not fall down from heaven. It is a human creation which attempts to interpret what is the real truth in a particular situation. In fact, it is based on the belief that appearances do not always correspond to reality. Things are not always what they seem, as the old song says. I do not think anyone would deny the wisdom of this insight. Nullity is just one instance of a broader approach to life which all of us would accept.

What nullity meant in the 'contract' approach to marriage was that, although the couple appeared to make a genuine contract of marriage, this was not in fact so. For some reason or other the contract was null. It might be because one or other partner lacked the requisite knowledge or freedom to undertake the contract of marriage. They might have had totally misguided ideas regarding what marriage is all about, or they might have been forced into marriage through the fear that something terrible would happen otherwise (e.g. threat of suicide). Another reason why the contract can be null is if some condition is added in implicitly by one partner which goes against the very substance of what they are committing themselves to. Or in some rare and bizaare cases the person one is marrying might not be the person one believed him to be.

For any of these reasons what appeared on the surface to have been a genuine contract of marriage might not have been so in reality. It is obvious that in this approach it is the partners' state of mind at the moment of entering the marriage which is put under the microscope. How the marriage worked out is far less important.

This approach still has its place in the marriage tribunal. To put the major emphasis on marriage as a 'relationship' is not to deny its character as a contract. It is simply to maintain that 'relationship' is more at the very heart of marriage than 'contract' is.

Does the 'relationship' approach to marriage have any bearing on the issue of nullity and the work of the marriage tribunals? It certainly has, even though I would suggest that it involves a much broader use of the term 'null'. Strictly speaking, nullity is a concept which is restricted to the field of contractual law. Only contracts can be said to be null. Relationships as such can hardly be said to be null. They can be non-existent, or non-viable, or even terminated, but to call them null is really to misuse language.

To be fair to the marriage tribunals, I imagine that they are blending together the two approaches to marriage. They are not applying the term 'null' to the relationship as such. Rather they are saying that if the relationship is a non-starter the substance of the marriage is not there and so the essential matter of the contract is missing. So the contract is obviously null.

This approach can be strongly defended and there is no doubt that very many people are being greatly helped by the work of the marriage tribunals. The marriage tribunal personnel have every right to claim that they are engaged in real pastoral work and their dedication is rewarded by the peace they help to bring to the lives of many people.

To recognize all that need not blind us to the incongruities of the system as it is currently developing. Many people involved in this field, including many tribunal personnel, are coming to the conclusion that a court of tribunal is the wrong form for helping people in the wake of marriage breakdown. Now that the emphasis has shifted to marriage as a relationship, what is far more appropriate is some kind of Marriage Counselling Service. Its task would not be to pass a judgement of nullity. Rather its task would be to help the people involved to arrive at an honest appraisal of their marriage relationship. Was it really viable in the first place? If not, are some of the reasons for this to be found in themselves and how will this affect future relationships? Did their relationship have a minimum viability, but somehow came to grief? Why did this happen and how can they learn from this? Is there any hope of re-establishing it? Is their relationship completely dead? Why has it died? Could they have avoided it and can they draw lessons for the future from this? What about the future? Is there a conversion process to be completed before they can face the future in peace? Have they the inner resources to accept a challenge of life-long celibacy or can they, for their own sakes or for their children, be open to the possibility of a second marriage?

I know that many tribunal personnel try to help people think through these problems. However, I would still query whether the tribunal is the appropriate setting for this kind of approach. The change of emphasis from 'contract' to relationship in marriage would seem to indicate the need for some major structural changes in the field of marriage care.

However, we have to live in the present so we need to be as clear as possible about the current situation regarding nullity of marriage in the Church today.

It is important to distinguish nullity from the juridical act of a declaration of nullity. When a marriage tribunal declares a marriage null it does not in fact make that marriage null. If it is right in its decision, the marriage is null already and has been null right from the beginning. The tribunal's declaration does nothing to change the marriage itself. Its value lies in its being a public and official act recognizing the already existing nullity of the marriage. In a certain sense a tribunal's decision is a very humble and almost diffident decision. It does not say: this marriage is null. It goes no further than saying 'We agree that this marriage is null' (constat de nullitate). Even when it gives a negative decision it refrains from declaring a marriage true and genuine. It will only say 'We do not agree that this marriage is null' (non constat de nullitate).

This obviously has important consequences for men and women who have suffered the tragedy of marriage breakdown and who with hindsight now believe that their first marriage was not a true marriage at all. The marriage tribunal offers them a service. Since they themselves are interested parties, it could be called a service in objective impartiality. This group of highly trained and experienced canon lawyers are willing to examine the first marriage and will give their opinion as to whether they think it was null or not. But in the end it is no more than their opinion. It does not change the truth of the situation. It is simply a professional but fallible attempt to discover the truth. If the ruling of the tribunal is that they are not convinced that the marriage was null, the couple have every right to stand by their own conviction that it was null as long as they are doing this in good conscience, really trying to discern what is the truth in the eyes of God.

It might be objected that, unless a person was a qualified canon lawyer or theologian, it would be very presumptuous for him to follow his own opinion in preference to that of the tribunal. After all, he would just be working on his own native wit, his intuition and his feelings – 'I just don't think that this is what marriage is meant to be'. I would suggest that the sound native wit and intuition of a good honest person deserves a lot of credence. Marriage tribunals are highly fallible institutions and I mean no disrespect by that. Increasingly they are becoming highly professional bodies, but quite naturally they are totally limited by the current situation in law and theology. This means that they have to keep to very strict rules regarding admissibility of evidence etc., and it also means that their criterion for finding the nullity of a marriage is determined by theological and psychological positions in current acceptance. All this is admirable and I do not mention it to criticise it. It is simply the natural limitation of a good human institution.

But it is a healthy reminder to us of the fallibility of this institution. For instance the very praiseworthy developments which are currently occurring in tribunal theory and practice mean that today very many marriages are being declared null which would not have been judged so ten or fifteen years ago. In effect, this means either that the tribunals are making thousands of wrong judgements today, or else that fifteen or so years ago very many marriages were null which had no chance of being declared so by a tribunal. Assuming that the latter is the case, this in turn means that it is possible that ten or fifteen years ago the intuition of the people involved in those marriages might have been a better guide to the truth than the professional judgement of the tribunals.

If that was true fifteen years ago, could it not still be true to some extent today, especially at a time when we claim to be learning so much about marriage from the actual insight and experience of married couples? It was Cardinal Hume himself who stated at the 1980 Synod that 'this experience and this understanding (of married people) constitute an authentic *fons theologiae* from which we, the pastors, and indeed the whole Church can draw' (*Briefing*, vol. 10, no. 32 p. 6). I am sure that no canon lawyer would claim that we have reached the end of the road in matrimonial jurisprudence, and that there will not be further developments in refining the causes for nullity in marriage.

It does not seem unreasonable, therefore, to believe that there are many marriages today which are in fact null and are thought to be 'not real marriages' by the partners involved, but which at present for a variety of reasons will not be able to be declared null by any marriage tribunal. It is encouraging to see this possibility recognized by the bishops of England and Wales: 'There are, however, other situations in which there may be moral certainty that the previous marriage was not valid even though this cannot be adequately established in the matrimonial courts' (*Easter People*, n. 111). If this is so, it would seem grossly unfair to dismiss as presumptuous a person who stood by his own intuition rather than by the judgement of the tribunal. In good conscience, such a person can genuinely believe that he is free before God to enter a second marriage. That is a belief which deserves respect from the rest of us. Such a person should certainly feel free to enter a second marriage and there should be no question of being refused the sacraments. At present Church law does not allow for any official public Church celebration of such a second marriage, but even among those who stand firm in the pre-Vatican II approach to moral theology it would seem acceptable practice for a priest to conduct a more private celebration of such a second marriage and to keep a record of it in a confidential register.

PAULINE PRIVILEGE, PAPAL DISSOLUTION AND THE 'RELATIONSHIP' APPROACH TO MARRIAGE

The Pauline Privilege and the exercise of the power of Papal Dissolution have in common the fact that what was considered to be a true marriage is considered to be no longer binding. I am including under Papal Dissolution the accepted law in the Church that solemn religious profession automatically dissolves a marriage as long as it has not been consummated. Most canon lawyers would interpret this as a general exercise of the power of Papal Dissolution. The Code of Canon Law (canon 1119) links with this the Papal power to dissolve the non-consummated marriage of baptized persons at their joint request, or even at the request of one partner in the face of the other's unwillingness. These instances of Papal Dissolution are very interesting, since they demonstrate that it is not the actual sacramental status of a marriage which makes it absolutely indissoluble in the eyes of the Church.

Expert canon lawyers dealing with this area of dissolution of the marriage bond make the point that it is justified on the grounds that 'The law of indissolubility is neglected in favour of a greater good, which is ordinarily the "salvation of souls"' (Abate, *The Dissolution of the Matrimonial Bond*, 1962). They quote Pius XII in their support: 'In every case, the supreme norm according to which the Roman Pontiff uses his vicarious power of dissolving marriage is . . . the "salus animarum", in the attainment of which not only the common good of religious society, and of human society in general, but also the welfare of individual souls will receive due and proportionate consideration' (*AAS*, XXXIII, 1941, p. 426).

All this would seem to be a filling out of Paul's original comment in 1 Cor. 7, 15: 'in these circumstances the brother or sister is not tied: God has called you to a life of peace'. Paul is saying something of deep significance there, and it is something which the Church has taken to heart in her limited practice of the dissolution of marriage. He is saying that the Lord's plan for marriage is one of love and peace. He has not called us to live at enmity with each other. If a marriage has no further future except at the level of constant bickering and fighting, and a kind of cold war neutrality, it can hardly be called a window on God's love which has called us to a life of peace.

The grounds for accepting that a particular marriage has dissolved seem clear enough, therefore. If they are to have a genuine Christian basis, it must lie in the moral impossibility for this couple to live together in peace. The 'relationship' approach to marriage finds no difficulty with this. As long as 'living in peace' is not interpreted superficially, ignoring all the ups and downs, trials and crises of any growing relationship, then it is fully in line with the 'relationship' approach. As currently interpreted by the Church there is a great difference between the Pauline Privilege and the various instances of the power of Papal Dissolution.

With the Pauline Privilege no act of jurisdictional power is considered necessary. The person simply is not bound by the first marriage and this 'being loosed' becomes reality, as it were, by the entry into the second marriage. This fits in perfectly with the 'relationship' approach. Provided the relationship is clearly dead (i.e. no possibility of living in peace), the first marriage no longer binds.

Papal Dissolution, however, brings in an additional element. As understood down through the ages, it requires an act of jurisdiction on the part of the Pope exercising the special vicarious power given him in his supreme office in the Church. In other words, when the Pope dissolves, God dissolves; and so his action does not contradict the words of the Lord 'What God has joined together, let no man put asunder' (Matt. 19,6).

It is at this point that the 'relationship' approach to marriage presents a major challenge. If the heart of any marriage is the personal relationship of life-giving love (which it is agreed is exclusive and permanent), then this is something which cannot be dissolved by any act of jurisdiction whatsoever. Sadly, as we well know, the relationship can dissolve and this can be due to both internal and external factors, but it certainly cannot be dissolved by any act of jurisdiction. Even God cannot give the Pope power to do that.

When the emphasis is put on marriage as a 'contract', there is no apparent difficulty. An act of jurisdiction can release people from a lawfully binding contract. In that context the notion of Papal Dissolution can make sense even though there may be other objections to it. But once it is admitted that the heart of a marriage lies in the couple's relationship, then the institution of Papal Dissolution loses its basic foundation.

If it is to continue to be exercised, it needs to be interpreted differently. It needs to be understood in the same kind of way as a declaration of nullity. In other words, all that the Pope can do is to recognize that the relationship has ceased to exist and so 'declare' that there is no longer any marriage. Consequently, at a public level he releases the two partners from the contractual legal effects involved in their marriage, though the natural rights of the children will obviously have to be safeguarded. If this is a correct interpretation of what actually happens when the Pope 'dissolves' a marriage, there would seem to be no reason why this 'declaratory' function should be reserved to the Pope. Since part of its role should be to make sure that a couple are not giving up too easily, it would seem more helpful if it took place at local level. It could be part of the pastoral function of the local bishop, who would probably be wise to delegate it to some kind of diocesan marriage counselling service, as mentioned earlier in this chapter. Such a service would obviously involve married people trained in counselling and with a sound understanding of the stages of growth in marriage.

'TWO IN ONE FLESH': A PERSONALIST APPROACH TO CONSUMMATION

Although the Church stands firmly by the truth that indissolubility is an essential property of every marriage, she has no difficulty in accepting that the marriages of non-Christians can dissolve and can cease to exist and be binding. This is an implicit admission that the human personal relationship of life-giving love (which the Church now acknowledges to be at the heart of marriage) can die. To admit this presents a major challenge to the way we have understood the indissolubility of marriage.

I think we have tended to evade the challenge by saying that the fact that the marriage of two Christians is a sacrament gives it a totally new depth of indissolubility and that renders it absolutely indissoluble.

Without wanting to deny what that statement is getting at, I think it is very unsatisfactory as it stands. For one thing, it ignores the fact that the Church has for many centuries claimed the power to dissolve sacramental marriages provided they were not consummated. This means that it is not the sacramental status as such which, in the Church's understanding, makes a marriage of two Christians absolutely indissoluble. According to the Church's practice it must be said that she identifies consummation as the key factor in making a sacramental marriage absolutely indissoluble. However, for most of her history in line with her belief that nature had designed intercourse principally for procreation, the Church regarded a marriage as being consummated provided that intercourse was performed correctly as a natural physical act open to procreation. It was not essential that the act consummating a marriage should be an act of love. In fact, it did not even have to be a fully conscious act. Amazingly, as recently as 1958 a Roman decision stated that a marriage was truly consummated even if one of the partners had to be drugged into unconsciousness to enable intercourse to take place. It stated that 'Consummation can be had independently of consciousness and free consent of the will' (*Canon Law Digest*, vol. 5, on canon 1119).

Along with many other theologians and canonists I cannot accept such an approach to consummation. I do not deny the basic insight that consummation has a bearing on indissolubility and I acknowledge that this intuition goes back to what Paul in Ephesians says about the marriage of two Christians and how their being 'two in one flesh' is a great mystery. However, I reject an excessively physical interpretation of being 'two in one flesh', even though I would not want to deny importance to the act of intercourse. It is a very significant element in the language of love between a couple. But being 'two in one flesh' is more than an interpenetration of two bodies; it is about two persons becoming one in a very real sense. According to this interpretation a marriage is consummated when the husband and wife really experience themselves as 'couple'. In other words, in their life-giving love for each other each has given and received so much that the words 'I cannot live without you' are no longer just an expression of the promise they have made, but an accurate summing up of what they now know from experience. When this experience is genuinely shared by both of them, their marriage can truly be said to be consummated.

When we are in the presence of a marriage which has been consummated in that sense, we are in the presence of something very precious and sacred. We are in the presence of the sacrament of marriage in the fullest sense of the word. The love of the Lord really is made visible in our midst in and through the love of such a couple. I hope I am saying this without romanticising it. There will still be pain and suffering, misunderstanding and hurt in their life together. That is not surprising since these were present even in the intimate love between Jesus and his Mother. But there will be an indissolubility in such a marriage, which really is a sacred image of the indissoluble love of Jesus for his Church. I am not claiming that the indissolubility of such a marriage could not possibly be broken, but I would say that to break it would be a sacrilege and must surely involve serious sin on the part of one or other partner. And I wonder whether such a marriage could ever really be dead and beyond all hope of reconciliation. And if the second union of one of the partners was the cause of this, I would find it hard to see how such a union could in any sense be something to be celebrated by the Church. If this sounds unduly hard, maybe it is because I believe that the Lord's love is so intensely present in a marriage which has achieved this degree of indissolubility that I scarcely believe it could be thwarted. Maybe that is how, within the 'personalist' approach to marriage, I rejoin the age-old belief of the Church that a sacramental marriage which is consummated is absolutely indissoluble.

However, not every sacramental marriage is consummated in this way and not everyone might be willing to accept this revised interpretation of consummation, even though a good number of canon lawyers and theologians seem to be saying something similar to this.

Even prescinding from this interpretation of consummation, is there anything else that can be said with reference to the statement that the fact that the marriage of two Christians is a sacrament gives it a totally new depth of indissolubility, and that renders it absolutely indissoluble?

Over ten years ago a very wise priest friend said something very thought-provoking. 'If the bread corrupts or the wine becomes totally diluted in the Eucharist, the real presence of the Lord is no longer there, since the sacramental species has ceased to be. If the heart of marriage (and so the matter of the sacrament of marriage) consists in the personal relationship of life-giving love, what happens to the sacrament of marriage if this relationship has become totally corrupted and has ceased to exist?' I can see no answer to that question other than that the sacrament of marriage has ceased to exist.

Such an assertion can sound very bland. 'A marriage was in existence; now it is gone. So what? Life must go on.' If that is all that is being said, a massive untruth is being perpetrated. No one would deny that the untimely death of a human being is a human tragedy deeply affecting many people. Although it may not be due to anyone's fault or sin, and although it is possible for good to come from it, it is certainly an evil.

Something very similar has to be said about the untimely death of any marriage; and it has an added dimension of evil and tragedy when it is the breakdown of the marriage of two

Christians. Despite its re-interpretation of the meaning of indissolubility, the 'relationship' approach to marriage does not play
down the evil of marriage breakdown. If anything, it enables us
to appreciate that evil even more starkly. Lady Helen
Oppenheimer expresses this very forcefully when she writes:

> Surely there is a real sin in putting asunder what God has
> joined, a sin which cannot be properly recognized by those
> who have to say that a broken marriage has not been put
> asunder at all, because either it is still in being or else it
> never was . . . The present suggestion is that a broken
> marriage is a broken marriage; something that stands out
> as an unnatural smashing of what was built to last, a
> blasphemy against the unity of Christ and his Church, an
> amputation inflicted upon a living body . . . The bond of
> marriage is indeed a real bond, affecting those who are
> joined in it for evermore. It can never be neatly untied, only
> harshly severed. When this injury has happened the prac-
> tical question is how the wound can best be healed, and the
> temptation is always either to cover it soothingly up at
> grave risk of it festering, or to keep it open for ever as a
> warning for others ('Is the Marriage Bond an Indissoluble
> "Vinculum"?' in *Theology*, LXXVIII, 1975, p. 242).

If according to this approach the first marriage has ceased to
exist, can a Christian choose to enter a second marriage? If he
really accepts the 'relationship' approach to marriage, then one
thing at least can be said in answer to this question. If as a
Christian he decides that he should not enter a second marriage, it cannot be because he believes his first marriage has
some kind of extra-terrestrial existence totally distinct from the
marriage relationship itself and that, thus existing, it still binds
him.

SECOND MARRIAGE – ADULTERY?

This question leads us straight back again to the two different
ways of understanding marriage which we looked at earlier.

Within the first pattern of marriage the Roman Catholic Church has clearly stated what is to be regarded as adultery. Moreover, by the various procedures already mentioned (nullity, Pauline and Petrine Privilege, dissolution of non-consummated sacramental marriage etc,) she has been able to classify as non-adulterous certain marriages which to an outsider might seem to be adultery, since they are second marriages while the former partner is still living.

However, we have already noted that, even for many who hold this first approach to marriage, these categories do not do full justice to their experience of the kind of second marriages under discussion in this chapter. They have encountered such marriages in which the couples are most certainly deeply loving spouses and parents with a deep Christian faith. This experience forces them to recognize that such marriages are truly vehicles of God's gracious love and it seems almost blasphemous to condemn them as adulterous. Of its very nature the term 'adultery' carries a negative moral evaluation. To call a marriage 'adultery' is not just to give a factual description of it; it is to pass a condemnatory moral judgement on it. That is why, in the various cases of permissible second marriage referred to above (i.e. Pauline and Petrine Privilege, nullity etc.,) the Church would never consider referring to them as acceptable or justified adultery. Instead she maintains that the first marriage was either non-existent or at least is no longer in existence.

A similar kind of approach is suggested by those who work from the second pattern of marriage; the relationship or covenant view. In the types of marriage breakdown under discussion they would claim that the first marriage never reached the state of achieved indissolubility; it was never consummated in a fully personal sense. It never really 'got off the ground' and it deteriorated to such an extent that it no longer exists. If the partners enter a second marriage, therefore, they cannot be regarded as being unfaithful to the first marriage since it has ceased to exist. Consequently, their second marriage is not classified as adultery. Obviously, how they stand as regards the law is a separate issue. That will be discussed later.

SECOND MARRIAGE – SACRAMENT?

Some writers today see the answer to this question as bound up with the debate as to whether for baptized Christians there can be a legitimate separation made between a natural marriage and a sacramental marriage. The context in which this debate has arisen is different from the issue under consideration in this book. It is the context in which a Church celebration of marriage is being asked for by two baptized Catholics who have now given up their faith and yet who still desire the solemnity of a Church wedding. The renewed appreciation of the necessity of personal faith for true sacramental practice poses a problem for such an arrangement. It makes it difficult to accept that a marriage can be viewed as a Christian sacrament when it involves two baptized Christians who no longer have any living faith in Christ, and for whom marriage has no Christian significance whatsoever. The 1980 Synod called for an investigation of this issue. The current practice of the Church is proving intolerable to many conscientious parochial priests. They feel themselves in an impossible dilemma. Either they take part in the seeming blasphemy of celebrating an apparently 'faith-less' sacramental marriage; or they refuse to marry the couple, knowing at the same time that the Church teaches that the couple cannot be married validly except before a priest and two witnesses. This pastoral problem has raised again the theological issue as to whether baptized Christians can contract a natural marriage without its being regarded as a sacramental marriage. In some areas such a distinction seems to be implicit in the pastoral policies being followed in an attempt to wrestle with this difficulty. These policies have the approval of the local bishops. For instance, in some parts of France and Switzerland the priest supports the couple through a civil marriage to which he might add some kind of blessing or moment of prayer; at the same time he begins to explore with them the Christian significance of their marriage in the hope that they might eventually be able to accept and celebrate it as a sacrament. It is suggested by some writers that this distinction between a sacramental and a natural marriage offers a solution to the problem of how the Church should regard second marriage after divorce. They would be true, natural marriages. It could be appropriate to bless them with a prayer since they belong to God's creation. But there would be no question of regarding them as sacramental and celebrating them accordingly.

I agree with those who reject this attempt to establish a two-tier system of marriage. Somehow it seems to miss the point of what is meant when marriage is said to be a symbol of God's love. While I share the concern of clergy who are profoundly worried about some of the marriages at which they officiate, I feel that at least in certain cases their worry is misplaced if it is focussed on the possible sacrilegious nature of what they are doing. If marriage really is a symbol of God's love, it can never be sacriligious to celebrate a true human marriage in church. In fact, the Japanese hierarchy are reported to have drawn up a rite of service for marriages of non-Christians, since they have received so many requests from such people asking the Church to help them celebrate their marriages as a sacred occasion. It is probably true to say that in some cases what priests are really worried about is not the couple's lack of faith, but their careless and immature approach to their forthcoming marriage. In such cases the word 'sacriligious' is hardly misplaced. To bless such a union in church is to attribute the sacredness of marriage to something which really has no claim to be called a marriage. But providing that a couple are really intent on a true marriage, priests should be only too happy to help them celebrate such a sacred occasion in their lives. Admittedly, their lack of faith in the person of Christ might demand some changes in the normal form of service, but that should not prevent the priest from helping them to appreciate as far as possible the sacredness of what they are doing. It is not the theology of marriage which opens a window on to God; it is the actual experience of marriage itself. Even if the priest does no more than help them to deepen their respect for the mysterious experience of life-giving love in which they are involving themselves together, he will be implicitly heightening their awareness of the experience of God in their married love.

In the end, as noted earlier, it is the human reality of marriage itself which is the substance of what the Roman Catholic Church calls the 'sacrament of marriage'. That is why I feel that the Church is so right in her teaching that the sacrament cannot be separated from the human reality. Consequently, if a marriage after divorce is to be accepted as a real marriage, it must be admitted that there is a sense in which it can also be said to be 'sacramental'. Sacraments are not only signs, but signs which bring about what they signify or symbolize: and they do not do that automatically. They can be effective signs in varying degrees. Presumably that is why Pius XI was willing to allow only a very restricted value as a Christian sign to a marriage not involving two Christians. In the case of a second marriage after divorce, it would be fair to say that its power to symbolize what a Christian marriage can be is to some extent impaired. Shared fidelity, which lies at the heart of marriage, can only be the joint creation of two persons. Therefore, in a second marriage after divorce one of the partners is bringing into the second marriage his or her personal history of failure in fidelity. This means that, viewed as a public sign or even as an experienced reality between the couple, there is a negative element present which makes the sign or the experience imperfect. The Eastern Church has catered for this by building into the celebration of the second marriage some kind of penitential element, though it seems that this is not always adhered to in practice. Something similar has been suggested for the Church of England, though many are opposed to it. Whether such a penitential note is present in the celebration or not, it is important to recognize that to accept the second marriage as sacramental does not imply that it should be put fully on a par with the first marriage from a sacramental point of view.

THE RADICAL, LIFE-GIVING TEACHING OF JESUS

Is this position an outright rejection of the clear words of Jesus in the New Testament? I do not think so. I would not for a moment claim that the original words of Jesus were anything but totally uncompromising. Any 'except' clauses appear to have been added by the Gospel writers to cope with pastoral problems in the early Church. Jesus refused to be drawn into the casuistic Rabbinical debate regarding when divorce might or might not be allowed because of the sinful situation created by the hardness of our hearts. His teaching was radical. It went right back to the roots or foundation of God's plan for marriage. He refuses to accept that divorce is part of that plan.

This teaching is not an intolerable burden laid on us. It is Gospel, good news. And it is good news that we urgently need today. There are people today who are claiming that to expect a man and a woman to pledge themselves to each other for life is to demand the impossible. Such a life-long commitment would be inhuman, they say. This is a message which is gaining credence and yet it is not a message which seems to bring deep happiness and it is certainly not a message that most people entering marriage want to hear. They embark on their marriage with the hope that they are going to share their whole lives together. For them the words of Jesus are good news. Your hope is really possible, he promises them. Life-long fidelity is a gift that is truly on offer to you. It is a grace, and God's grace is freely given. But the Church in her wisdom reminds us that grace must build on nature. Life-long fidelity is a gift freely available to us – but it is also a task to which we must apply ourselves. If we want really to live, we must accept the pattern of dying and rising.

Jesus proclaimed his radical, life-giving teaching on marriage in the terms imposed by the thought-categories of his own age and culture. These must have been his own thought-categories. Dr Dominian's elaborate analysis of the phases of growth in marriage would have been quite foreign to him, as would any talk about nullity or papal dissolution. It is surely not irreverent to say that today we know far more about marriage and growth in marriage than Jesus knew. For him divorce could only be thought of within the category of human sin and so any remarriage after divorce had to be condemned as adultery.

Fidelity to the teaching of Jesus does not oblige the Church to remain locked within the thought-categories of his time and culture. In fact, the Church today can only be truly faithful to his teaching by presenting it enriched by the best insights of our own age and culture. This does not imply any dilution of his teaching. Today the radical teaching of Jesus must become incarnate within our new way of understanding marriage.

For Jesus divorce was a positive action by which one partner (usually the man) sent away the other. Divorce was an action which repudiated the contract of marriage and which treated the other partner unjustly. As such it could only be thought of within the category of human sin and so any remarriage after divorce had to be condemned as adultery. All the complexities of growth in marriage, with the subtle role of sexuality within that growth, would have been a foreign language to Jesus. Despite his great compassion towards all who were wounded and in need of healing, he would not have been able to see marriage breakdown as a terrible human tragedy which left people desperately wounded and in great need of healing. This would not have been blindness on his part. It would have been because marriage breakdown in his day and in his culture would have been a different human reality to what it is today in our Western culture. Despite his welcome for people who were categorized as sinners and made outcasts by the community, he would not have seen anyone who gave his marriage partner a bill of divorce in that light. Jesus would see such a person as acting out the hardness of his heart. He would probably be angry with him as he was with the scribes and Pharisees. But for us today many who suffer the tragedy of marriage breakdown are often victims of sin rather than perpetrators of sin.

Jesus could not see that way in his own day because things were different then. But he does see that way now – in and through us, and in and through his Church. Our task is, as it were, to let his heart shine through our eyes. We must not sell our age short by minimising the radical challenge and invitation in the teaching of Jesus. But neither must we deny our age the compassion of Jesus by closing our eyes to those whom we can now recognize as deeply wounded and in great need of healing and bringing back to life again.

There must be a two-way process going on, therefore. There must be an interpenetration of the radical teaching of Jesus and the best insights on marriage available in our own day. We do not preserve the treasure of the faith by burying it as the man in the Gospel buried his one talent. That is wasting it and letting it die and stultify. To use a phrase of the Pope when still Archbishop Wojtyla, to defend and preserve the deposit of the faith 'entails its growing understanding, in tune with the demands of every age and responding to them according to the progress of theology and human science' (quoted in *Theological Studies*, 1979, p. 96). Therefore, simply to accept the new understanding of marriage on its own is not enough. Somehow it must be enriched by being infused with the radical teaching of Jesus. Unless this happens, the Church is merely repeating the teaching of secular experts on marriage. While what they say may be extremely valuable and must be listened to and received respectfully by the Church, it is still not the Gospel. A further question has to be asked, therefore: what does the radical teaching of Jesus imply with regard to indissolubility as it is made incarnate in the new way of understanding marriage? The radical demand of Jesus does not add some new ingredient to marriage. It is not creating a new reality called 'Christian marriage'. Rather, it is reminding men and women of the deeper significance of marriage. This natural human reality of marriage involves the mysterious process by which distinct persons become one in a very real sense even though they retain their distinctness and individuality. This 'oneness in communion' language is familiar to the Christian. It occurs in the one-in-threeness of the Trinity, in the person Christ being truly man and God, in the one Church being a communion of churches, in the one body of Christ being made up of many members, in the one vine having many branches etc. Oneness in communion is seen to be at the very heart of God himself and the whole of reality seems shot through with this hallmark of God.

It is seen most clearly in the sphere of personal relationships, among which marriage has a very special and unique place. In rejecting divorce on the grounds that 'it was not so from the beginning', Jesus is propounding teaching which is truly radical. That is, he is going back to the real roots of the indissolubility of marriage. The oneness in communion in marriage is a symbol of the oneness in communion of God himself. In other words, through this human experience a couple gain a glimpse of what God is like and actually share in his love. And in reverse, since the oneness in communion of marriage is itself a reflection of God's oneness in communion, a new light is thrown on marriage itself. This oneness in communion, if it is to be true to its roots, cannot be merely transitory. It is only fully authentic if it achieves a permanence which reflects the faithfulness of God himself. This applies to all marriages, not just to the marriages of Christians.

Jesus is recalling *all* married couples to their origins. What is really new, however, what is 'revelation', is Jesus himself who in his person is the oneness in communion of God with man. In his person he is the sacrament of oneness in communion between God and man; and his body, the Church, is called to continue this sacramental presence and mission throughout history. That is why, if marriage today is to be true to its roots, it must reflect the fidelity of oneness in communion revealed in Christ and his Church. This does not demand a new kind of fidelity from marriage, but it does open our eyes to a new dimension of fidelity in marriage. The couple's faithful love is not only a deep and very privileged aspect of their being an 'image of God' and a sharing in his love. It is also a 'real presence' of the faithful love of Christ himself. This makes us even more aware of just how precious is the human reality of faithful love in marriage. This realization by itself does not cause married love to be any more faithful. That can only come from the growth and development of the human reality of married love itself. That is why the only way to make the radical teaching of Jesus really effective within today's understanding of marriage is by giving top priority to fostering the growth and development of this human reality of life-giving, faithful married love. It can hardly be said to be a top priority unless the following challenges are accepted and faced up to:

1. An initial challenge to the Church (and to society in general) to demonstrate its faith that married couples really are

capable of such God-like oneness in communion, by providing the helps needed to enable their marriages to reach the state of inner indissolubility. In other words, the first challenge is to the community, rather than to individuals.

2. A challenge to all couples to prepare properly for their marriage and to really work at it once they are married, making full use of all available resources, internal and external. This is not a lack of faith in each other or in their marriage. Grace builds on nature. Normally speaking, they can only hope to enjoy the faithful love they are invited to share if they are prepared. to take all the human steps necessary to safeguard and develop it.

3. A challenge to those who are enjoying the fruit of achieved indissolubility (i.e. their marriages are sacramental in the full sense of the word) to accept their mission in the Church to share this gift with other married couples by helping them in their turn to reach and become confirmed in a similar personal indissolubility.

4. A challenge to the Church to recognize that it is marriage breakdown itself which goes counter to the oneness in communion in which we reflect and share in the life of God himself. It is not the legal divorce nor even the second marriage. These both come afterwards. What is really against oneness in communion in marriage is the slow corrosive process by which the relationship gradually deteriorates and finally dies altogether. To the extent that the Church recognizes this, she will be able to concentrate her efforts on the educational, supportive and remedial work needed to sustain fidelity in marriage; and she will not feel the same need to penalise those who have been unfortunate enough to have lost this pearl of great price, whether through their own fault or through force of circumstances beyond their full control.

5. A challenge to couples to recognize that growth in fidelity will only normally occur through phases of crisis and that in a very special way in their marriage each will have to live the

Gospel invitation of losing self in order to find the true self. This inner conviction of faith that the cross which leads to new life will be experienced within marriage should provide the inner strength and conviction to keep going in times of darkness.

This final point is important and deserves further elaboration. It is frequently said that any change in the Church's policy in the direction of admitting the divorced-remarried to the sacraments would deprive married people of an essential support in their moments of crisis. They need a strong external law to sustain their fidelity in the difficult times of inner weakness. Without it many couples would easily give up the struggle and they would miss the opportunity of allowing a crisis-point to develop into a growth-point in their marriage. This may well have been true formerly. It would seem to be less true today. This may be because nowadays more people are experiencing marriage, at least implicitly, according to the pattern of the new understanding of marriage. If this is true, the crisis situation which formerly was so well catered for by the strong law has to be catered for in some equally effective way within the new approach to marriage. As suggested above, this will be provided for at two levels: first, by the local Church (and particularly by loving married couples within the local community) being alert to the needs of married couples in these crisis times, and being actually organized to provide any external help needed; and second, by the couples, through adequate preparation, being more aware of the nature of these crises and thus being helped to cope with them and experience them in faith as transition phases to a new level of relationship.

CONCLUSION

By comparing today's experience and understanding of marriage with that which was widely accepted until very recently, this chapter has come to the conclusion that these two views result in two different interpretations of indissolubility. It is difficult to see how these two positions can possibly be reconciled. This is not to suggest that the former position cannot be updated to some extent so as to incorporate at least some appreciation of marriage as growth in relationship. Neither is it to suggest that the position I am proposing does not appreciate the important role of law in safeguarding the good of marriage. However, when it comes to the critical issue of marriage break-down and the possibility of remarriage, it is there that the two views go their separate ways. Nevertheless, it would be unfair for either position to accuse the other of not really believing in the indissolubility of marriage, even though each might be tempted to think that the other is failing to concentrate on the central core of the issue.

If they cannot be completely reconciled, are they available as two alternative positions within the Church, or at least for the Church? Although at first sight that might seem an attractive way out of the impasse, I feel it is not a solution open to the Church. The Church is committed to interpreting the Gospel in the light of the best insights available to her in any age, even though in the process she must always keep one eye on the way earlier Christians have undertaken this same task. It would seem that the current best insights on the human reality of marriage leave the Church no choice but to accept the new position. In fact, it could be argued that the official acceptance of the change-over to this position is implied in the approach to marriage adopted by Vatican II in *The Church in the Modern World*.

I firmly believe in the indissolubility of marriage and I also believe that the Church must never fail to uphold this, even though, as stated earlier, I prefer the more personalist term of 'life-long fidelity' to indissolubility. If I became convinced that the position outlined in this chapter denied that truth, I would not hesitate to renounce it. To reinterpret indissolubility in the light of the Church's richer understanding of the human reality of marriage should not be construed as a denial of indissolubil-ity. In fact, it is trying to unearth the full riches of this precious gift of faithful married love in order that it can be better appreciated and lived out in today's world.

3

SACRAMENTS FOR
THE DIVORCED-REMARRIED
– THE THEOLOGICAL ARGUMENTS

The rest of this book is concerned with the possibility of Holy Communion for Catholics who are involved in a second marriage after divorce, either because their own first marriage has broken down or because they have married one of the partners of a broken marriage. Though this and the following chapter come naturally after our discussion of indissolubility, it is worth noting that the position I am about to develop does not depend completely for its validity on the interpretation of indissolubility I have suggested in the previous chapter. As already mentioned, in the world of theological writing there seems to be a fair measure of agreement with the main lines of the position expressed in this chapter, whereas there has been far less discussion of how the modern approach to marriage affects our understanding of indissolubility.

I would also like to stress that this chapter is focusing on just *one* of the needs of those in a second marriage. It is the need felt by many in this situation to share more fully in the sacramental life of the Church. In the actual everyday life of the Church and of the local Christian community this need cannot be viewed in isolation from the many other important human needs of such people (eg their need for acceptance, practical support, legal and financial aid, help with the children, involvement in the community etc). If these needs are ignored, there is a danger that the sacraments will be experienced merely as religious actions with no relevance for nor roots in the ordinary life of the community. Nevertheless, the sacramental question can and needs to be examined in its own right. The Church has a growing concern for the pastoral care of the divorced-remarried as regards all their other needs. But when it comes to their sacramental needs, there she draws the line.

Many people find this hard to understand. It gives the impression of an unsympathetic and unforgiving Church who does not really understand what these people have been through and who cannot in her heart of hearts bring herself to fully accept them. In this sense, the sacramental question becomes for many a test of the Church's credibility. If the Church cannot cope with marriage breakdown today, she cannot cope with life; and so it becomes hard to believe that she is the sign of God's love for all men and women in the world of today.

Therefore, this chapter will deal with the theological question: can the Catholic Church allow to the sacraments those who are involved in a second marriage after divorce?

It is a basic principle of Catholic pastoral theology that no one should be refused the sacraments unless he or she is manifestly unworthy or would give grave scandal or is barred from the sacraments by the Church. This chapter will examine whether those in a second marriage after divorce are manifestly unworthy or whether grave scandal would be caused by their receiving the sacraments. The next chapter will consider whether they are forbidden the sacraments by any law or teaching of the Church; and, if so, what is its current binding force and should it be changed?

ARE THEY 'LIVING IN SIN'?

Until recently most Catholics would have said that couples in a second marriage after divorce are 'living in sin'. Many of the couples themselves would have accepted that, at least in theory. What was meant by this expression was that the couple were living in 'a state of mortal sin'. In other words, the sin in question was personal sin. They were alienated from God.

Personal sin?

Though there are still many Catholics who would view such couples in this way, it is not the position which is adopted in most of the more recent official statements in the Church. And it is rarely found even in those contemporary theologians who are still unable to accept their admission to the sacraments. Their writings frequently imply that God's grace may be alive and active in the lives of these people and they nearly always encourage such couples to develop their prayer life and to share in the Church's mission and worship, short of receiving the sacraments. This is very beautifully expressed in the authoritative Chapter 11 of the 1980 French pastoral directives. It speaks of them 'building an authentic spiritual life, inspired by the Spirit and rooted in hope in God who never abandons those who trust in him.'

The recent utterances of Pope John Paul II are more ambiguous. He too insists that the divorced-remarried 'do not consider themselves as separated from the Church, for as baptized persons they can, and indeed must, share in her life' (*Familiaris Consortio*, n. 84). He calls on the whole Church to encourage them to be actively involved in all aspects of the Church's life. Yet at the same time he insists that they need sacramental reconciliation and that this must be refused to them unless they radically change their way of life. This sounds very harsh and condemnatory teaching but is softened somewhat by the Pope's describing their situation as *'objectively* contradicting that union of love between Christ and the Church which is signified and effected by the Eucharist'. In this he seems to pull back from passing any judgement on their inner personal stance in love before the Lord. Certainly the advice to be actively involved in the prayer and missionary life of the Church is hardly consistent with the judgement that the couple are at enmity with God and living in a personal stance of mortal sin.

A living contradiction

This is probably why there has developed another way of presenting the 'living in sin' argument. This is not directly concerned with the personal state of the couple, how they stand before God. It is using the word 'sin' almost in the sense of 'contradiction'. Marriage is about faithful love, whereas a second marriage after divorce contradicts faithful love. So such a second marriage is really a living contradiction.

At first sight, the new way of presenting the 'living in sin' argument might seem to be simply another way of saying that their second marriage is wrong but they are in good faith about it. However, I think it is saying more than this. It is talking about couples who are fully aware of the Church's current teaching that their second marriage is wrong. Yet they are deciding that in their particular situation it is right for them to remain in this marriage. To maintain that they are 'in good faith' is not a satisfactory explanation since it implies that they do not know that what they are doing is wrong. They do know that the Church teaches it is wrong; yet they are also convinced that it is right for them. This might sound like double-think. But it is a fair description of the state of mind engendered among many Catholics by the Church's approach to morality in recent centuries.

Making a right decision: the law of gradualness
In fact, it was precisely this state of mind (though in the context of the contraception debate) that the bishops in the Synod were addressing themselves to when they found great help in what they called 'the law of gradualness'. The law of gradualness refers to the kind of dilemma situation in which two different points of focus have to be kept in view even though for the present they cannot be fully aligned with each other. The first focus (it could be called the 'universal' focus) is the universal value or law which is concerned with the good of human persons in general and which challenges the individual regardless of his particular situation. The second focus (the 'particular' focus) involves both the individual's capacity at this stage in the history of his personal development and also any features in his particular situation which may have special human significance. The law of gradualness is directed towards a growing alignment of the particular with the universal focus. However,

it accepts that the 'particular' focus will be the determining one when the individual comes to make his personal decision at this point in time in this specific situation. Nevertheless, there will always be something unsatisfactory about any decision in which the 'particular' and the 'universal' focus cannot be properly aligned together. The law of gradualness recognizes that this process of alignment takes time; it is a gradual process. In the case of certain individuals or in some particular circumstances, perhaps it will never be open to more than a partial achievement. Certain values may never be able to be achieved, however gradually, by some persons unless there first occurs some change in the situation in which they have to live their lives and this might be beyond their control and might never occur in their lifetime. Incidentally, the discrepancy between the two points of focus would be roughly the equivalent to what contemporary moral theologians would refer to as 'non-moral evil'. That is their way of recognizing that there is something unsatisfactory as long as both foci are not aligned. However, they would insist that the law of gradualness must not be restricted to the subjective field of inner personal development. The personal sphere cannot be divorced from its social context. Pope John Paul rightly warns against an abuse of the 'law of gradualness' which would take all creative tension out of a humanly unsatisfactory situation (one which is not properly focussed) by saying that each situation is virtually independent and has its own law. This would be tantamount to extreme 'situation ethics' and would receive no support from contemporary Catholic moral theologians.

What might seem a highly theoretical discussion is in fact very relevant for the issue of people living in a second marriage. The law of gradualness is a way of saying that people can only start from where they are. That is where their decisions have to be made. And where they are includes their present stage of development on all levels; emotional, psychological, intellectual, moral and spiritual. What is demanded of them is not some super-human decision totally beyond their present capabilities. What is asked of them is a decision which according to their own capacity is rightly made i.e. gives due importance to the most important values insofar as they see them. Moreover, as already noted, part of starting from where they are involves starting from their present interpersonal and social situations.

Bearing all this in mind I would have no hesitation in saying that entering a second marriage or (even more so) remaining faithful to an already existing second marriage can certainly be envisaged as a *rightly made* decision for many Catholics. And if it is rightly made, I think it can also be described as the right decision for them (i.e. in their present state and at this particular moment in time within this specific situation). And if it is in this sense the right decision for them, it is accurate to describe it as morally good.

If that is the case with regard to the second marriage decisions of many Catholics, it is not appropriate to use the term 'sin' in any sense to refer to their marriages. That is not to deny that there is evil involved in their second marriage situation. But this is not moral evil. It is what many theologians today would refer to as 'non-moral evil'. The evil in question is the regrettable fact that their second marriage is not and cannot be fully aligned to the important focal point of life-long marital fidelity. The term Pope John Paul uses to describe this evil is 'objective contradiction'.

Living in contradiction to the Eucharist

This leads us on to the changed emphasis in the 'living in sin' argument. It has now developed into a 'living in contradiction to the Eucharist' argument. In the Eucharist we celebrate the indissoluble love of Christ for his Church. And the marriage of two Christians is called to be a symbol and living presence of that love. That is why earlier in this book I embraced Helen Oppenheimer's description of the evil of marriage breakdown: 'a blasphemy against the unity of Christ and his Church'. This being so, a strong case can be made out for describing a second marriage after divorce as a living contradiction to the Eucharist. Certainly it is living witness that the faithful love of the first marriage is no longer in operation.

In one of their propositions to the Pope, the Synod bishops state: 'They cannot be admitted to eucharistic communion since

their status and way of life *objectively* contradicts the indissolubility of that covenant of love between Christ and the Church
which is signified and actualised by the Eucharist' (Proposition
14, n. 3). The Pope obviously took their words to heart since in
his recent Apostolic Exhortation, *Familiaris Consortio*, he has
written: 'They are unable to be admitted thereto (i.e. to Eucharistic Communion) from the fact that their state and condition of
life objectively contradicts that union of love between Christ
and the Church which is signified and effected by the Eucharist'
(n. 84).

The argument that the divorced-remarried must be refused
Holy Communion because they are living in objective contradiction to the Eucharist was put forward by the International
Theological Commission in its 1978 statement. It is echoed in
the statements of the Italian and French bishops. As far as I can
ascertain it is only in recent years that the argument for necessary exclusion from the Eucharist has been articulated in this
way. It is an argument which I used myself in *The Clergy Review*,
1970, pp. 123–141. As will be clear in what follows, honesty
now forces me to say that I am no longer convinced by it as an
argument *necessitating* exclusion from the Eucharist.

An unconvincing argument for exclusion
The question to be faced is: what is the force of this 'living in
contradiction to the Eucharist' argument? I do not think that the
contradiction can be really denied, but does it entail exclusion
from Holy Communion as a necessary consequence? By way of
parenthesis it might be noted that since this 'living in contradiction to the Eucharist' form of the argument does not presume
sin in any personal sense (although it does not deny its possibility), the sacrament of reconciliation would not seem to present an insuperable obstacle at the level of pastoral practice.

Roman Catholic theology of the Eucharist has developed
considerably in recent years. Many of the liturgical changes
introduced by Vatican II are the fruits of this development. For
instance, today far more emphasis is laid on the fact that we
celebrate the Eucharist as a community. It is seen as a celebration in which the whole Christian community have their

part to play. And the Christian community itself is seen less as a gathering of the saints and more as a coming together en route of the pilgrim church in which all are at the same time saints and sinners. This is one of the points high-lighted by the bishops in their post-Congress document, *The Easter People*, n. 22. Every Eucharist significantly begins with a short service of confession of sinfulness and grateful acceptance of forgiveness; the communicant's final words before receiving are 'Lord, I am not worthy . . .' Moreover, 'full, conscious and active participation' is seen by Vatican II to be demanded by the very nature of the liturgy and is to be regarded as 'the aim to be considered before all else' (Liturgy Constitution, n. 14). Furthermore, the Council also speaks of the Eucharist as having a twofold meaning and purpose: it should be both a sign of unity and a means to unity (cf. Decree on Ecumenism, n. 8).

It is the development in Eucharistic theology that has enabled the Church to open the way to allowing non-Catholic Christians to receive the Eucharist in certain situations. As long as we look at the Eucharist exclusively from the angle of its being a sign of unity achieved, it is difficult for us to understand how non-Catholic Christians can be admitted to the Eucharist since their objective status contradicts that unity. But once we open our eyes to the Eucharist as a means to achieving unity the impossibility vanishes and we even become more humble in acknowledging our own contribution to disunity in the Church.

In the light of this current understanding of the Eucharist, an absolute prohibition of communion to the divorced-remarried can hardly be claimed to be a necessary theological conclusion and the pastoral wisdom of maintaining such a prohibition needs to be seriously questioned. For one thing it lays too much emphasis on the Eucharist as a sign of already existing community and it ignores the power of the Eucharist in helping us to achieve a greater unity. It also turns a blind eye to the many ways (small and great) in which the lives of other members of the community might be out of focus; in fact, a conclusion of the view I am criticising could well be that the main body of the Church in the so-called 'developed' West should not be admitted to communion because it is involved in structural (i.e.

objective) injustice vis-a-vis the third world! The Justice Sector of the Pastoral Congress had the humility to confess this on behalf of the Church in this country but the bishops in *The Easter People* did not draw the conclusion that we should all be put under an interdict!

Furthermore, to recommend the divorced-remarried to attend the Eucharist without communicating seems contrary to the participation demanded by the very nature of the Eucharist. Likewise, the pastoral advice sometimes given that they might receive the sacraments in a church where they are not known seems to conflict with our understanding of the Eucharist as the celebration of *this* (usually local) community.

All this would seem to point to the conclusion that it is a theological exaggeration to state that the couple's admission to communion would totally contradict the meaning of the Eucharist and so is impossible. On the contrary, the understanding of the Eucharist in contemporary theology could produce equally strong arguments in favour of their admission.

WOULD THEIR RECEIVING THE SACRAMENTS CAUSE SCANDAL?

Maybe this Eucharistic argument which I have been criticising is merely a theological superstructure erected as a defence of a very practical and understandable concern of the Church. This would be the Church's concern to uphold the indissolubility of marriage because it believes this is necessary if the institution of marriage is to be preserved and the happiness of married people safeguarded. For instance, the section of Proposition 14 of the Synod referred to above continues: 'Furthermore, there is a special pastoral reason (i.e. why they should not be admitted to communion), namely, because this would cause the faithful to be misled and confused about the Church's teaching on the indissolubility of marriage'.

Once again the Pope makes these words his own in *Familiaris Consortio*, n. 84. Perhaps, then, the basic reasons for the absolute prohibition run along lines such as the following: so that people will not be misled into thinking that the Church is no longer committed to indissolubility; so that those struggling with crises in their marriage will not give up but will be supported in their struggle by the Church's unambiguous witness; so that those entering marriage will really accept that they are pledging themselves to a life-long commitment etc. If these are really the fundamental concerns underlying the theological argument, then that argument is the same as the 'scandal' argument. Let us now examine that argument in more detail.

Scandal – arguing from consequences

This maintains that the strength of the Church's witness for indissolubility will be weakened by allowing these couples to the sacraments. As a consequence of this, more marriages will end up in the tragedy of breakdown. In this sense, by such a practice the Church would be implicitly helping to spread the evil of marriage breakdown. That would be a scandal in the true meaning of the word. It would be leading others into evil and perhaps even into personal sin. That is an argument based on consequences. How can it be proved true or false? Short of actually implementing the suggested policy for a period of time on an experimental basis (and even that would hardly provide convincing proof), the only ways of testing the validity of the scandal argument would seem to be:

a) Investigate situations where this policy has been in operation already e.g. some local communities in the Roman Catholic Church; other Christian Churches who have followed a similar policy.
b) Investigate whether there are any experimental findings drawn from parallel situations which might be helpful.
c) Look more closely at the scandal argument itself in order to evaluate its internal strength as an argument.

To the extent that the first two investigations are feasible, it is important that they should be undertaken. Ultimately, there is no real substitute for sound experimental data in considering an argument from consequences. However, since I do not have access to such experimental data and since such investigations would be beyond my field of competence, I have no option but to restrict myself to the third choice. I hope that others might be able to carry out the investigations mentioned. If they do, I look forward to learning from their findings.

A question of priorities

The scandal argument states that, if she were to admit such divorced-remarried people to the sacraments, the Church would be contributing to the increase in marriage breakdown. The basic premise of this argument seems to be: the Church must not do anything which would contribute to the increase in marriage breakdown. This sounds very convincing and it might seem to be a statement which no Christian could question. Nevertheless, it does need to be looked at more closely. Should it be accepted as an absolute rule? Or should it be interpreted merely as emphasising a value which ought to be given a high priority? If the former, then the Church can never allow anything to overrule it. Yet in fact the Church does weigh it in the balance with other values. For instance, the group whose marriages are most at risk are those who marry under the age of twenty-one, especially when there is a pre-marital pregnancy. The Church could make a law prohibiting such marriages. However, she refuses to do this because of the respect she has for another basic human value, that of human freedom. She is therefore willing to contribute to the breakdown of marriage through her act of omission (i.e. not forbidding such marriages by law) because she fears that such legislation would violate this other basic human value of personal freedom.

Therefore, to say that the Church must never do anything which would contribute to the increase in marriage breakdown does not seem to be completely accurate as a statement of the Church's position as revealed in her practice. A more accurate statement might be: because the Church is very conscious of the great evil involved in marriage breakdown, she will do all in her power to lessen this evil and she will try to do nothing to contribute towards it insofar as this can be reconciled with her concern for other basic human Christian values.

To look at how convincing the scandal argument is, therefore, we need to look at two questions related to it. The first is: is refusal of the Sacraments the most effective way to bear witness to the Church's belief in the indissolubility of marriage and thus help to prevent more marriages from breaking down? The second is: is there another important value at stake which might justify the Church in adopting a pastoral policy which might in the eyes of the world weaken her stand on indissolubility?

Witnessing to a belief in the indissolubility of marriage

Before she takes a stand against anything, the Church must always stand for something. In other words, she must be committed to some positive human and Christian value which she sees to be threatened by this negative phenomenon. In the instance we are examining, the Church stands for life-giving and life-long faithful love in marriage. She cares deeply about this value because she cares about people and this value is intimately bound up with the deepest good of people. People's true happiness is at stake here. Love is God's greatest gift to humanity and the Church is concerned that love be genuine and true to itself. In fact, through this precious human reality a window is opened, allowing men and women to get a glimpse and an experience of what God himself is like.

It is this concern for true life-giving and faithful love in marriage which makes the Church so strong in her determination to safeguard people from the pain and suffering of marriage breakdown. That is why she refuses to weaken in her belief in the indissolubility of marriage.

However, it is fair to ask whether refusing Communion to the divorced-remarried is an effective way of giving this witness. Paradoxically, the people who are most convinced about the evil of marriage breakdown and who have the deepest belief that life-long faithful love is one of God's most precious gifts, are those who themselves have been through the painful agony of marriage breakdown. They have experienced in their own persons its dehumanising effects. They have seen at first hand the shattering impact it has on their children. If the Church really wants to mobilize a body of people who see how precious is the gift of faithful love in marriage, she could make a good start by enlisting all those who have been through the tragedy of marriage breakdown. The fact that some of them have remarried could hardly be used as an argument against their belief in the goodness of life-long faithful love. In fact, this belief has probably been part of their motivation in remarrying. They want to find that precious gift which eluded them in their first marriage.

In terms of public witness, therefore, refusal of Communion comes over to people more as a form of punishment and victimization. I honestly believe that the Church would be more effective in combating marriage breakdown if she made the divorced-remarried feel completely at home at the table of the Lord and from there drew them into active involvement in the apostolate of preparation and support for marriage.

In the end, the only effective way the Church will overcome the evil of marriage breakdown will be by making the marriage apostolate a top priority in her pastoral policy. In fact, until recently it could be argued that a major scandal was the fact that the Church gave such a low priority to the kind of work needed to enable marriages to become truly indissoluble. Through her sins of omission in this field it could even be argued that the Church has actually contributed greatly to the breakdown of marriage. However, it is probably unhelpful to labour this point since, after all, the Church can only do her best within the limits of her understanding of marriage at any point of time. The law of gradualness even applies to the Church herself, though I am tempted to complain that she has been far too gradual in giving proper recognition and realistic support to a major prophet in this field, Dr Jack Dominian.

Nevertheless, what can hardly be denied is that if the Church today is to be a credible witness standing for the indissolubility of marriage, she must give a real (and not just notional) priority to the kind of pastoral care which will be needed if marriages are to become indissoluble in fact rather than just in theory. As Paul VI wrote in *Evangelization in the Modern World*: 'Modern man listens more willingly to witnesses than to teachers, and if he does listen to teachers it is because they are witnesses' (n. 41).

Thank goodness, things have been changing in recent years.

With a richer appreciation of marriage as a process of growth in relationships, there has been a move to introduce into the Church's pastoral policy an emphasis on training and support during the initial phases of growth and development. The Catholic Marriage Advisory Council has led the field in this area with their educational, pre-marriage and remedial work. In the past few years a particularly important contribution has been made by the Marriage Encounter movement and this shows every sign of being a major influence for good in the years ahead.

Perhaps this change of emphasis in pastoral policy could be linked with two approaches to marriage and indissolubility discussed in the previous chapter. The change could be described as a shift from an external to an internal emphasis. The external approach would say: we believe in the indissolubility of marriage and we show this by our absolute stand against divorce and remarriage and by our refusing the sacraments to the divorced-remarried. The internal approach would say: we believe in the indissolubility of marriage and we show this by the high pastoral priority we put on doing everything possible to help marriages become really indissoluble.

The value of healing and forgiveness

There is another aspect of scandal which needs to be considered. In many instances, it would be truer to describe those whose marriages have broken down as victims of sin rather than as perpetrators of sin. Certainly, many will emerge from the traumatic process of marriage breakdown as wounded people. They are men and women needing help and healing, not judgement and condemnation. It should be a scandal if the Church were to turn her back on them in their time of need since she is committed to doing all in her power to bring healing to hurt and wounded people. Many people whose marriages have broken down come into that category. They have been through a form of dying and they need help if they are to be brought back to life again and if they are to find real healing. Obviously, the question arises: can this new life and healing come through entering into a second marriage? I have no doubt at all that this can and does happen in a fair number of cases. Clearly such a statement would carry far more weight if it had the backing of some good research into the healing potentiality of second marriages. Careful research into this field might make it possible to draw up some kind of picture of the healing process after marriage breakdown. This could be helpful in discerning whether a prospective second marriage might offer genuine healing or whether it might simply be leading into a repetition of what went wrong in the first marriage. It might also help towards a deeper appreciation of the special needs of those for whom healing will have to be found in living singly or as single parents.

If a second marriage brings true healing, and especially if for some men and women it is the only way of finding true healing, I feel that the Church has no choice but to accept it as good. 'Is it against the law on the sabbath to do good, or to do evil; to save life, or to destroy it?' (Luke 6, 9). To deny healing in the name of God's law comes perilously close to the position of the Pharisees which Jesus opposed so strongly.

The need for repentance
The thrust of the Church's pastoral care is always in the direction of healing and forgiveness. Obviously, therefore, the need for inner repentance and forgiveness must be given a high priority. If a marriage reaches the stage of irreconcilable breakdown, although that means that resumption of married life is now impossible, it does not mean that there is no need for some form of reconciliation and forgiveness. Both partners should be ready to accept responsibility for any ways in which they contributed to the breakdown of the marriage, and to the extent that this was due to their deliberate fault they should be sincerely sorry for it. In their hearts they must also want to forgive the other for his or her share in the breakdown process with all its attendant sufferings to both of them and to the children.

Although the English law has dropped the distinction between the 'innocent' and 'guilty' party in a marriage breakdown and although it is probably true that both partners share responsibility to some extent in every breakdown process, never-theless at the level of personal responsibility before God perhaps it would be unrealistic to ignore these categories altogether. Especially when we are dealing with marriages which seem to have been real marriages and which no one is claiming to have been null, the breakdown process may have begun in some instances through factors within the control of one or other of the partners. Consequently one or other might carry a greater responsibility for the breakdown of the marriage. In that case it might be fair to think of that person as the 'guilty' partner and the other might be more sinned against than sinning. If this is true, it has implications both at the level of scandal caused in the community and at the level of the quality of repentance and forgiveness needed.

This distinction needs to be kept in mind in any consideration of pastoral practice. In instances where it would seem appropriate to speak of a 'guilty' and an 'innocent' party, some kind of differentiation of practice would seem to be indicated. This is obviously in the thoughts of Pope John Paul II reflecting the mind of the Synod:

> Pastors must know that, for the sake of truth, they are obliged to exercise careful discernment of situations. There is in fact a difference between those who have sincerely tried to save their first marriage and have been unjustly abandoned, and those who through their own grave fault have destroyed a canonically valid marriage (*Familiaris Consortio*, n. 84).

In the case of a 'guilty' partner, for a pastoral practice to respect the needs of healing and forgiveness, some additional requirements such as the following might seem to be indicated:

a) a sincere desire for the innocent partner's forgiveness and willingness to change as far as possible whatever in the present situation is hurtful to the innocent partner.

b) an appreciation of the scandal he has caused in the local community and a determination not to do anything that might increase that scandal still further. This might mean that even though he is sincerely repentant, he might judge that his receiving the sacraments would further disturb and disrupt the community rather than express and increase communion. And so at least for a time he might voluntarily but regretfully refrain from receiving the sacraments. When the public celebration of the sacrament of reconciliation becomes more confidently re-established in the life of the Church, perhaps that might provide the context for celebrating the reconciliation of one who had caused such public scandal in the local community.

The individual and the public good

I am not denying that on occasion individuals have to suffer to avoid much greater harm being done to people in general. Nor am I denying that willingness to give one's life for others is a hallmark of the disciple of Jesus. But it does not follow that those who have suffered the human tragedy of marriage breakdown should be forced (or should be willing) to carry their cross to the end by accepting the loneliness of a life of non-chosen celibacy. That would only follow if it could be proved that their not remarrying would certainly help others to avoid the tragic suffering they themselves have been through. Unless that were proved, it would be unjust to put moral or legal pressure on such people to sacrifice their personal well-being for a cause which might be completely unfounded. It is true that restrictive laws can be made to avert probable dangers to the common good, and this is precisely why it is reasonable to have civil and ecclesiastical legislation governing the area of marriage breakdown and second marriage. Nevertheless, such laws must not restrict individual liberty beyond the needs of the common good. Increasingly, civil legislation is judging that some level of acceptance of second marriage is on balance beneficial rather than harmful to the common good. If this judgement is well-founded, the Church cannot but take note of it if she is going to employ the same criterion of concern for the common good.

CONCLUSION

The position outlined in this chapter is totally different from what is called a 'divorce mentality'. That is a vision of marriage which would see no particular value in life-long fidelity. In fact, some versions of it would even claim that the pledge of life-long fidelity is a denial of human freedom and turns marriage into a life-sentence rather than an occasion of personal enrichment for both partners.

The 'divorce mentality' would, therefore, see nothing harmful or evil in marriage breakdown. It would see it merely as a perfectly normal phase in the transition from one close friendship to another.

According to the way of understanding marriage which I have been proposing, irretrievable marriage breakdown is definitely seen as an evil. It is not in accord with God's plan for human living and loving. And to the extent that its causes can be laid at the doorstep of human responsibility, it can truly be regarded as the fruit of sin. To what extent any particular breakdown can be attributed to the personal sin of the couple themselves is quite a different question. Yet even when it would seem to be principally due to their sin and they themselves are willing to accept this humbly and in a spirit of repentance, it is not regarded as an unforgivable sin. Consequently, if, as is being assumed here, their repentance cannot take the form of the resumption of married life together, and if they subsequently find healing through entering a second marriage, there are no convincing grounds for saying that they cannot be admitted to the sacraments. Neither the 'living in sin' argument nor the 'scandal' argument prove the case against admission to the sacraments.

4

SACRAMENTS FOR THE DIVORCED-REMARRIED – WHAT CAN WE DO IN PRACTICE?

The previous chapter considered the theological question: *can* the Catholic Church allow those in a second marriage after divorce to receive the sacraments? The answer was 'Yes'. This final chapter will move to the level of practice. In other words, the question now becomes: *may* those in a second marriage after divorce receive sacraments in the Catholic Church? This in turn will need to be broken down into three separate questions:

a) Does the Catholic Church forbid them the sacraments?
b) If so, how strictly should this prohibition be interpreted by such couples themselves and by those who administer the sacraments?
c) Would a divergent practice lead to pastoral chaos?

It should be noticed that in what follows I am constantly referring to the 'divorced-remarried'. Obviously, for most practical purposes my remarks apply equally to those who are not themselves divorced and remarried but who have married a divorced person.

DOES THE CATHOLIC CHURCH FORBID THE SACRAMENTS TO THE DIVORCED REMARRIED?

The impression has been given throughout the second part of this book that the Catholic Church does forbid the sacraments to the divorced-remarried. However, what this means needs much closer examination. At a popular level virtually all Catholics believe that the divorced-remarried are forbidden to receive the sacraments. Is this belief correct? Does the Catholic Church forbid the sacraments to the divorced-remarried? Within the Catholic Church a prohibition can arise from two different sources. It can come from the Church's law or it can flow as a direct consequence of the Church's doctrinal or moral teaching. This division is not meant to suggest that the Church's laws have no grounding in her doctrinal or moral teaching. It is merely recognizing that not everything which is regarded as forbidden in the Church needs to have a special Church law made against it.

Not excommunicated
Many Catholics think that the divorced-remarried are excommunicated. Even more tragically, some of the divorced-remarried themselves believe this to be true and this has caused them to drift away from the Church. In fact, whatever other reasons might be offered for their not receiving the sacraments, all experts in Church law would agree that there is absolutely no question of the divorced-remarried being excommunicated in the proper sense of that word.

Not forbidden by Church law
Although not all experts in Church law would agree with it, a strong case can be argued for saying that the category of divorced-remarried men and women under consideration here are not forbidden by any Church law to receive the sacraments. This involves a highly technical legal argument which is based on detailed analysis of the Church's laws dealing with non-admission to the sacraments. It would be out of place here to try to spell out all the points of the argument and the objections of those who reject it. For the purpose of this book it is enough to note that this interpretation is sufficiently well-founded to bring into play the accepted principle that 'a doubtful law does not bind'. In other words, because there is sufficient doubt whether any prohibition exists in law against such people receiving the sacraments, for purposes of practical decision making no obligation should be presumed to exist. Conse-

quently, if it is held that the Catholic Church forbids the sacraments to the divorced-remarried, the source of this prohibition must be sought in her doctrinal and moral teaching since it is not enshrined in her laws.

This is an important distinction. It means that if any such prohibition exists, it should be interpreted according to the principles of moral theology and not of Church law.

Not forbidden by theology

In the previous chapter it has already been shown that such a prohibition is not a necessary consequence of our contemporary theological understanding on marriage and the Eucharist. In fact, current developments in theology in both these areas would tend to point in the opposite direction. They would seem to indicate that in the kind of divorce-remarriage situation under consideration it would be more appropriate to admit them to the sacraments rather than refuse them.

OFFICIAL STATEMENTS OF AUTHORITATIVE TEACHING

However, it cannot be denied that at the level of official Church teaching it is quite clearly taught that such couples should not be admitted to the sacraments. Pope Paul VI spoke in this vein and the same position is expressed by the International Theological Commission (1978) both in its own statement and in a paper by G. Martelet to which it gave general approval. The Congregation for the Doctrine of the Faith has adopted the same position in its dealings with some bishops' conferences, particularly in its letter from Cardinal Seper sent to the bishops in 1973. Pope John Paul II's closing address to the 1980 Synod reiterates this position, as does his Apostolic Exhortation, *Familiaris Consortio* (1981).

Public proclamation and pastoral practice

Although all these statements seem to present a total and absolute prohibition, it is worth noting that some commentators who have studied the Vatican's style of dealing with such matters would argue that this is far from being the case. Such statements need to be interpreted in the light of the Roman approach to moral theology which makes a distinction between moral principle and pastoral practice. According to this view, if a principle is to have any real effectiveness, it must be stated clearly, unequivocally and without any qualification. Provided this is done, there is then room for some flexibility in pastoral practice. It is claimed that this approach has been drawn from the standard writers in moral theology in recent centuries. Consequently, even the apparently uncompromising letter of the Congregation for the Doctrine of the Faith could be understood as giving a hint of a much more liberal approach in its cryptic footnote, 'Consult the approved authors'. This could also explain why the Congregation for the Doctrine of the Faith has given what seem to be unnecessarily ambiguous answers to very clear questions put to them on this matter.

Put very crudely, this approach means that authority says a very clear 'No' to the possibility of the divorced-remarried receiving the sacraments but this unambiguous 'No' is intended only for the purposes of public proclamation. It is meant as a clear public witness of the Church's commitment to indissolubility. But it is not intended as a guide for pastoral practice. Pastoral practice operates on a different level altogether and is the concern of pastoral theology. This is the level at which guidance has to be offered for the difficult process of decision-making in a situation where other values besides indissolubility have also to be considered and where all the particularities of an individual's stage of personal growth and his unique situation have to be taken account of. An instance of this two-tier approach was quoted in *The Clergy Review* a few years ago. In 1975 the Sacred Congregation for the Doctrine of the Faith issued a document entitled *Declaration on Certain Questions concerning Sexual Ethics*. In its treatment of homosexuality it shows a good grasp of the issues at stake and tries to tackle the pastoral problem with compassion and sensitivity. However, it insists that 'According to the objective moral order, homosexual relations are acts which lack an essential and indispensable finality' and it states that 'homosexual acts are intrinsically disordered and can in no case be approved of' (n. 8). It is common knowledge that one of the co-authors of this declaration was Fr Visser C.Ss.R., professor of moral theology at Propaganda Fide. One of Fr Visser's colleagues makes the following comment about his approach to homosexuality:

> As a moral theologian he has no doubt in categorically stating that homosexuality is intrinsically immoral. A homosexual relationship just does not make sense in terms of principles, and therefore it is always intrinsically wrong. But when he comes to deal with the person who is homosexual, Fr Visser's one concern is to help the person to live as stable a Christian life as possible in his situation. In an interview in the magazine *L'Europa*, on 30 January, 1976 (after the publication of the Declaration) Fr Visser said 'when one is dealing with people who are so deeply homosexual that they will be in serious personal and perhaps social trouble unless they attain a steady partnership within their homosexual lives, one can recommend them to seek such a partnership, and one accepts this relationship as the best they can do in their present situation'. Fr Visser justifies this on the grounds that the lesser of two evils is often the best thing for people in a particular situation and that one can pastorally and positively recommend the lesser evil as the best thing here and now. He would see no incompatibility between such a pastoral attitude and the adherence to the general, abstract principle that homosexual acts are always intrinsically evil (Sean O'Riordan, 'The "Declaration on Certain Questions concerning Sexual Ethics"' in *The Clergy Review*, 1976, p. 233).

Naturally, the Anglo-Saxon mind finds this approach quite foreign and difficult to understand. It smacks of double-standard morality and can easily lead to a loss of credibility of the Church's moral teaching. Despite our dissatisfaction with this approach, we have to bear it in mind when we are trying to interpret to what extent the authors of these official statements intended them to be understood at the level of practical decision-making.

Divergent voices among the bishops

The 1979 statement of the Italian Episcopal Conference probably belongs to the same type of expression as these official Roman statements. This is not the case with the very delicately worded pastoral letter issued in 1979 by the bishops of the French-speaking cantons of Switzerland or with the equally sensitive pastoral directives of Bishop LeBourgeois of Autun some years previously. From these and from various first-hand and second hand reports of initiatives being taken in some dioceses or regions I have gained the impression that the practice of admitting some groups of the divorced remarried to the sacraments is growing in various parts of the Church, and that it is receiving some level of informal approval from a number of bishops either individually or even in groups. Unfortunately, I have found it impossible to gather any official documentation on this point.

The 1980 Roman Synod on Marriage and the Family

However, the views voiced by various bishops in the 1980 Synod are a good indication that there is a desire in some countries that a way should be found to permit the divorced-remarried in some circumstances to receive the sacraments. In fact, one of the forty-three Synod propositions handed over to the Pope includes a request that the practice of the Eastern Church in this matter should be closely studied. The Eastern Church's notion of 'economy' tries to accommodate the demands of the Gospel within the reduced possibilities of the imperfect situation following marriage breakdown. Remarriage is usually allowed but it is not put on a par with a first marriage. This is an ancient practice in the Eastern Church and must be accepted as part of the Christian heritage we share in our diversity. This was acknowledged at the Council of Trent. Canon 7 of Session XXIV which appears at first sight to be a hard-line approach on indissolubility allowing no possibility of remarriage, was in fact very carefully worded so as not to offend

Christians of the Eastern Rite. Very deliberately it refused to state that their divergent practice did not have equal claims to be founded on the Gospel and tradition. Furthermore, a recent study has suggested that this practice of the Eastern Church had a certain counterpart in the West for many centuries: those in a second marriage were allowed to continue living together as man and wife once they had done the penance required by the Church.

It is obviously the hope of the Synod that we in the Roman Catholic Church might be able to learn something from this ancient practice in the Eastern Church.

Another part of the Synod proposition already referred to recognizes a great difference between those whose marriage has broken down despite their real efforts to make it work and those who by their sinful conduct have actually destroyed their marriage. 'Out of love of the truth pastors are obliged to discern between such situations.'

Pope John Paul II

This is a theme which is taken up and expanded by the Pope in *Familiaris Consortio*, n. 84:

> Pastors must know that, for the sake of truth, they are obliged to exercise careful discernment of situations. There is in fact a difference between those who have sincerely tried to save their first marriage and have been unjustly abandoned, and those who through their own grave fault have destroyed a canonically valid marriage. Finally, there are those who have entered a second union for the sake of the children's upbringing, and who are sometimes subjectively certain in conscience that their previous and irreparably destroyed marriage had never been valid.

The Pope does not say what this discernment means in practice. Perhaps it is a veiled reference to the kind of pastoral guidance offered by pastoral theology and so stoutly defended by Fr Visser. If it is, it would explain the rather puzzling statement at the end of the Pope's treatment of divorced persons who have remarried, where he says that the position he has adopted shows the Church's 'motherly concern for these children of hers, especially those who, through no fault of their own, have been abandoned by their legitimate partner.'

I do not share the views of those who believe that the remarks of Pope John Paul II in his closing address to the Synod have put paid to any developments in this direction. A careful analysis of what he actually said is most revealing. In the first place, he received all forty-three propositions 'as a singularly precious fruit of the works of the Synod' and he even called them a 'rich treasury'. There are no grounds for thinking that he excluded the Synod's concern for the divorced-remarried from these words of praise. Moreoever, when he moved on to speak specifically about the question of the divorced-remarried and the sacraments, his remarks were phrased in such a way as to give the impression that he was not adding anything new of his own but was merely articulating for the Synod Fathers what seemed to be their own mind on this matter. He summed this up in three points:

1. The Synod reaffirmed the Church's practice of not admitting to communion the divorced-remarried.

2. Those who come into this category should be given special pastoral care by 'Pastors and the whole Christian community'.

3. It must not be denied that they can receive the sacraments if they show sincere repentance by living as brother and sister and if there is no scandal.

Respect for the Synod and consultation
It could easily be interpreted as the Pope's final decision that there must be no change in this matter. I feel that is too pessimistic an interpretation. Pope John Paul II knew well enough the alternative solutions which were being proposed in the Church. As he sat through the Synod debates he had heard some of the bishops arguing that these alternative solutions should be given serious consideration.

One of the strongest of these pleas came from Archbishop Worlock. He was not speaking purely as an individual. He spoke out of the experience of listening to groups of committed Catholics at parish level all over England and Wales discussing this issue. The consensus from such discussion comes over clearly in the summary of the Diocesan Reports prior to the National Pastoral Congress:

> Almost every report makes an urgent plea for a re-examination of present policy on this matter (admission to the sacraments for divorced and remarried people). A new pastoral strategy should come from the bishops, with special consideration of the spiritual needs of divorcees.
>
> People cannot understand the rigidity of the Church in this regard: 'Jesus would not refuse to come to them. The Church forgives anything, even murder, but not remarriage': this feeling is echoed in many reports.
>
> Reports ask for . . . a blessing on the second marriage (*Liverpool 1980*, p. 68).

This same conviction was repeated in the Congress itself:

> They (the bishops) should look at ways of showing compassion to those whose marriages have broken irreconcilably, whose second marriage is a living witness to Christ and who seek to re-establish unity with the Church through the Eucharist (*Liverpool 1980*, p. 173).

In *The Easter People* (n. 109) the bishops showed themselves not unsympathetic to these pleas but it was Archbishop Worlock who gave them most eloquent expression in his powerful intervention in the presence of the Pope during the opening week of the Synod:

> Yet despite our best efforts, some marriages fail and family unity is destroyed. To these victims of misfortune, not necessarily of personal sin, or of sin which has not been forgiven, the Church, both universal and local, must have a healing ministry of consolation.

Moreover, many pastors nowadays are faced with Catholics whose first marriages have perished and who have now a second and more stable (if legally only civil) union in which they seek to bring up a new family. Often such persons, especially in their desire to help their children, long for the restoration of full eucharistic communion with the Church and its Lord. Is this spirit of repentance and desire for sacramental strength to be for ever frustrated? Can they be told only that they must reject their new responsibilities as a necessary condition of forgiveness and restoration to sacramental life?

Some pastors argue that the Church's teaching on marital fidelity and contractual indissolubility are here at risk. They fear lest other Catholics would be scandalised and the bond of marriage weakened. Our pre-synodal consultation would question this assertion. Those who vigorously uphold the Church's teaching on indissolubility, also ask for mercy and compassion for the repentant who have suffered irrevocable marital breakdown. There is no easy answer. But our Synod must listen seriously to this voice of experienced priests and laity pleading for consideration of this problem of their less happy brethren. They ask that the Church should provide for the spiritually destitute to the same degree as it strives today to meet the material needs of those physically starving (*Briefing*, vol. 10, no. 32 p. 8).

By calling the Synod the Pope was trying to implement the process of consultation and shared responsibility in the Church. It is worth noting that with regard to the National Pastoral Congress he congratulated the Church in England and Wales 'for the initiative you are taking in shared responsibility' (*Liverpool 1980*, p. 108).

It would be contrary to the spirit of the Synod and a denial of the Pope's commitment to it to suggest that in his closing speech or in *Familiaris Consortio* he was simply putting a stop to an on-going process of reflection, consultation and shared responsibility. It seems to me that he was merely stating what was a fact, namely, that the Synod could not bring itself to take the step of reversing the Church's current official position. That is entirely different to uttering a definitive statement declaring the matter closed for now and for ever. I prefer to look on the Pope's statement as a holding operation. The current debate will continue. Pressing pastoral problems will still have to be faced and solved at local level. But for the moment the *official* position in the Church still holds, even though, as mentioned earlier, there are grounds for believing that at the level of practice the official position might be far more flexible than might appear at first sight.

Living as brother and sister

Perhaps a word should be said about the so-called 'brother and sister arrangement' which the Pope states is a required sign of repentance for a couple who for serious reasons are unable to separate. It might be thought that this is insisting on a requirement found in the traditional manuals of moral theology. This is not quite true. Although it is mentioned as a possibility in most of the pre-Vatican II moral theology text books, it is usually accompanied by the caution that it should rarely, if ever, be recommended to a couple. In fact, in the very rare instances where the authors would see it as being a possibility, they add in conditions which belong to another age and which would be impossible for most people, with the current housing situation.

Furthermore, more serious objections can be raised against the 'brother and sister arrangement'. This arrangement demands, in the words of the Pope, that the couple 'take on themselves the duty to live in complete continence, that is, by abstinence from the acts proper to married couples'. If it is the relationship itself which lies at the heart of a marriage, this is a strange requirement. It insists on the non-practice of one aspect of marriage but allows what constitutes the heart of marriage to remain. It allows a couple to continue loving each other faithfully but it forbids them to express that love in the language of sexual intercourse. Moreover, it is totally ineffective as a measure to obviate what is considered to be a public scandal and a counter-witness to indissolubility. In the public eye such a couple will be remaining as they were, continuing to live together as man and wife. I know of no moral theologian, however pre-Vatican II, who would insist that a couple in this situation should make a public declaration that they are only living together as brother and sister. And if they made such a declaration I would suspect that it might well cause even greater scandal!

The Synod and concern for human persons

One important point comes out strong and clear from the Synod. In their approach to marriage the bishops were primarily concerned about the good of persons and so they were deeply committed to fostering and supporting loving relationships in marriage. It was this same concern for persons which was the guiding spirit in their discussion of the divorced-remarried and it is this attitude that the bishops want to share with the Church at large. The Synod offered no support for those who would argue that man is made for the sabbath and not the sabbath for man; laws are to service the good of persons, not to be a burden crushing them. If we are going to err in any direction, it seems to me that it is more in line with the climate of the Synod to err in the direction of pastoral openness towards persons seeking healing for the wounds of marriage breakdown. I draw support from the fact that, if the approach I have adopted in this book is erroneous, at least it errs in the direction in which the spirit of the Synod is pointing. The Pope's closing words on the subject of the divorced-remarried clearly show the direction he would like the Church to take during this holding operation: 'Meanwhile the Church, praying for them and strengthening them in faith and hope, must show herself a merciful mother towards them.'

In the light of all this we need to face the following question: as long as the official position of the Church remains as it is at present, how strictly should the prohibition of the sacraments to the divorced-remarried be interpreted?

HOW STRICTLY IS THIS PROHIBITION TO BE INTERPRETED?

Widespread rejection of theological and pastoral grounds for refusing communion

Since this prohibition is not enshrined in any Church law, but is upheld by Church authorities as a *necessary* consequence of the Church's understanding of marriage and the Eucharist, it would seem that the degree of its obligation depends to some extent on whether this 'necessary consequence' view is correct or not. We have seen already that weighty reasons against it can be drawn from the Church's current understanding of marriage and the Eucharist. I am not alone in thinking this. One only needs to look through the theological and canonical journals of the last decade to realize that the majority of theologians and canonists writing on this subject reject the view that the Church has no choice but to maintain such a prohibition. Two years ago I sent a questionnaire round all those teaching moral theology to seminarians in England, Ireland and Scotland. Out of the 26 replies received, 21 favoured a more open practice (involving the sacraments under the kind of conditions I mention in the following pages); they said that such a practice was in accord with sound theology and that even now they would be prepared to follow it themselves in appropriate circumstances. 3 took the opposite view and 2 felt unable to give a definite answer. Nor are these the views of isolated individuals. The French Association of Teachers of Moral Theology have agreed that a milder practice is both theologically possible and pastorally desirable. A similar conclusion was reached by a sub-committee of the Catholic Theological Society of America and by a working party set up by the Canon Law Society of America. An Austrian commission chaired by Cardinal Koenig also favoured a more open pastoral policy, even though there was no final consensus on the moral and theological reasoning in favour of it. Furthermore, in the course of various meetings with different groups of lay-people over recent years I have found that what theologians are saying at a professional level corresponds to what many good married Catholics feel should be happening. It is not that they reject the Church's teaching as too demanding. In a sense, they see it as not demanding enough: it is too unbending at the level of negative prohibition but too undemanding at the more positive level of personal investment in the process of preparing for and developing the growth of relationship in marriage. The desire voiced by the National Pastoral Congress for a more open pastoral policy towards the divorced-remarried seems to have been a faithful expression of the voice of many Catholic men and women.

Therefore, if it is true to say that the degree of the obligation of the current official prohibition is linked to the validity of its theological basis, it seems to me that the widespread questioning of this theological basis implies that its obligation is *qualified* rather than absolute.

The decision of responsible dissent

In recent years all Catholics have been forced to accept the fact that at least for others, even if not for themselves, a situation can arise when one has to resolve a dilemma in decision-making due to a conflict between what remains the fallible teaching of the Church and what one believes oneself. It is accepted teaching that within certain limits the dissenting decision of such a person can be a fully responsible Christian decision and should be recognized as such by his fellow-Catholics. He should in no way be branded as a disloyal Catholic for taking this stand. It is being assumed in this teaching that such a person is basing his dissenting judgement on serious reasons, usually shared by others in the Church; and it is also being assumed that he remains sufficiently open to admit that, since in any such situation of divergence it is unlikely that an adequate expression of the truth has yet been reached, it might be necessary for him to revise his position at a later date.

This is not just a question of intellectual dissent which has no bearing on life. It means dissent which justifies a person's acting in apparent contradiction to the official teaching. Obviously, the relevance of this teaching which has a long pedigree in Catholic theology, came very much to the fore after the publication of *Humanae Vitae*. Shortly before *Humanae Vitae* was issued, this teaching was given a thorough airing in a magisterial document issued by the German Hierarchy. Since *Humanae Vitae* it has been reinforced by many other hierarchies in their pastoral guidelines to help married couples with decision making in the wake of the encyclical. A good example is found in the statement of the Scandinavian bishops:

> Should someone, for grave and carefully considered reasons, not feel able to subscribe to the arguments of the encyclical, he is entitled, as has been constantly acknowledged, to entertain other views than those put forward in a non-infallible declaration of the Church. No one should, therefore, on account of such diverging opinions alone, be regarded as an inferior Catholic. Whoever, after conscientious reflection, believes he is justified in not accepting the teaching and not applying it in practice, must be answerable to God for his attitude and his acts (Horgan edit., *Humanae Vitae and the Bishops*, p. 238).

A much fuller version of this same teaching is found in the statement of the Canadian bishops and is quoted in the Appendix to this book.

This position can sound very much like an extreme form of 'follow your own conscience' and might appear to be completely individualistic and totally opposed to the common good of the community. Far from it, however. It presumes that the individual believes in the community and is concerned about the truths and values to which the community is committed. Moreoever, it presumes a person who, as a Christian, believes that the Lord's Spirit is active in the community, helping us to discern the truth in action. It was this kind of presumption which enabled the Pope (then Cardinal Wojtyla and writing as a phenomenologist philosopher) to describe this stance of dissent as 'essentially an attitude of solidarity'. In the section of his book *The Acting Person* (Reidel, London, 1979) which deals with what is needed for any human community to be healthy, he stresses that opposition is vital to any community's growth and well-being. 'The one who voices his opposition to the general or particular rules or regulations of the community does not thereby reject his membership' (p. 286). In fact, it is an obligation on the community to recognize the constructive role of loyal opposition and to structure itself to enable this to be effective:

> In order for opposition to be constructive, the structure, and beyond it the system of communities of a given society, must be such as to allow opposition that emerges from the soil of solidarity not only to *express* itself within the framework of the given community but also to *operate* for its benefit. The structure of a human community is correct only if it admits not just the presence of a justified opposition but also that practical effectiveness of opposition required by the common good and the right of participation (pp 286–7)

For many of us brought up to believe in a doctrine of absolute obedience to all human authority and particularly to Church authority, the notion of responsible dissent might seem hard to swallow and a denial of all that we have held dear in our tradition. In fact, it has a very solid basis in tradition, especially in the thought of St Thomas Aquinas. It also has a good pedigree in our native culture in England and Wales. To deny responsible dissent in theory or in practice is to take the path that leds to totalitarianism. No doubt that is why Cardinal Wojtyla, writing in the context of Poland, was able to see the need for it so clearly.

In practice

Applied to the situation under discussion, the notion of responsible dissent would mean that a Catholic who is involved in a second marriage after divorce could in certain circumstances be making a fully responsible Christian decision in presenting himself for absolution or Holy Communion. The kind of conditions which most writers would regard as essential if such a decision is to be genuinely responsible are the following:

1. The first marriage is irretrievably broken down and there is no possibility of its being restored again.

2. All obligations in justice towards the other partner and the children of the first marriage are being fulfilled as far as is humanly possible.

3. The second marriage is being lived in good faith. In other words, it is being experienced as 'What God wants us to do'. This might seem a very vague statement and hardly the equivalent of the 'serious reasons' mentioned above. However, the theologian, Karl Rahner, has argued convincingly that in an area of human experience such as marriage and in a climate of open theological discussion, such a way of putting it could be a genuine expression of the same truth that others are expressing in more theological language.

4. The desire for the sacraments must be motivated by genuine faith. One would hope that this could normally be presumed to be the case.

Nevertheless, the presence of these conditions is not the end of the matter. The reception of the sacraments needs a minister. It is one thing for an individual to dissent from the official teaching of the Church and to follow his own conscience. But that does not give him the right to violate the conscience of the minister from whom he is requesting the sacraments. Anyone administering the sacraments does so in the name of the Church whose minister he or she is. Does not that imply a special obligation of fidelity to the official teaching of the Church?

It does in the sense that if such a person is exercising a teaching function in the Church he has a duty at least to present the official teaching as well as he can, even though this does not release him from his duty in honesty to express any important reservations he may have about this teaching, if he deems this appropriate. However, that is a completely different matter from refusing the sacraments to someone with the kind of dissenting conscience referred to above. He should not consider himself duty-bound to refuse such a person the sacraments. This is implicit in the teaching of a number of episcopal conferences in their pastoral commentaries on *Human Vitae*. As already mentioned, in this they are not propounding new teaching; they are simply repeating and applying the traditional teaching of the 'approved authors'.

DOES RESPONSIBLE DISSENT OPEN THE FLOOD-GATES AND LEAD TO PASTORAL CHAOS?

Eliminating genuine scandal

What about the situation when a person whose matrimonial situation is truly scandalous and is causing serious dis-edification in the local community asks for the sacraments on the grounds that he is in good faith and is merely following his conscience. In such a situation most priests would try gently but firmly to change his alleged 'good faith' into 'bad faith'. This would merely be exercising that aspect of their pastoral minis try which is called 'judgement' by the Old Testament prophets and which today might be better described by the phrase 'healing diagnosis'. This might take time, of course, but in the meantime few priests would have any qualms about firmly but kindly refusing such a person the sacraments. If a person is manifestly causing public scandal, both truth and compassion demand that he be challenged to face this, so that he can be helped to repentance and true healing. This would be an example of the 'discernment' that the Synod bishops were referring to. In an extreme case, the local bishop might have to be called upon to intervene, rather in the way that a doctor would call in a second opinion.

Opening the flood-gates

It might be objected that once the right to a dissenting con-science is acknowledged in this area, the flood-gates would be open and all the divorced-remarried would be queuing up for the sacraments. I do not think for one moment that that would happen but, for the sake of argument, let us suppose that it did. Would this be a major disaster? I must confess that I would not be at all dismayed if all the divorced-remarried who fulfilled the conditions outlined earlier returned to the sacraments. And even if there were some who did not fulfil all the conditions, their hunger for the sacraments would be a healthy starting point for helping them to see what still needs to be done. I feel it is closer to the spirit of the Gospel to rejoice at such a happening than to lament at it. The latter attitude would be reminiscent of that of the elder brother in the parable of the prodigal son.

Responsible dissent and celebrating a second marriage

In Chapter II I argued that in some instances a second marriage after divorce can be acknowledged as good and even, in a restricted sense, as sacramental. Does this mean that there is no problem about celebrating such a marriage in Church?

This brings us back again to the question of Church law and public pastoral policy. The official celebration of marriage is an official act within the Church. As such it is governed by Church law which is drawn up by the legitimate authorities with the common good and public order in mind. Clearly it is beyond the competence of any individual minister to change the public law of the Church. While it is true that a dissenting conscience can on occasion be sufficient justification for the non-observance of law, such a conscience cannot confer the jurisdiction required by law for certain official acts. In this area of second marriage, therefore, a priest could not claim legitimate jurisdiction for his action if he officiated publicly at a second marriage after divorce while the first marriage is still recognized by the Church as valid. However, the couple in such a situation might with reason feel justified in not observing the Church's law by getting married in a registry office.

In the preceding remarks I feel that I have introduced a note of caution which seems inconsistent with the rest of my line of argument. Perhaps it would be more consistent to acknowledge that in a very exceptional case a priest might be acting responsibly in agreeing to celebrate in Church a second marriage after divorce. Maybe a distinction needs to be made between the liturgical significance of such a celebration and its juridical validity. The fact that no official validity could be claimed for it would not automatically empty it of all liturgical significance. Maybe my unwillingness to entertain the possibility of a Church celebration is simply a sign of my own lack of courage and my natural cautiousness. There is little doubt that to act in this way would sometimes put a priest in dispute with his bishop and perhaps also with many Catholics in his parish. Although that would not prove that his action was not justified, yet these are factors which cannot be dismissed as irrelevant. While it is true that Christian witness will often provoke opposition, it is also true that peace in the community is a matter of Christian concern, even though it should not be interpreted as peace at any price. Certainly I would have no hesitation in saying that if a priest believes that a person is making a genuine decision of responsible dissent in entering a second marriage, he should feel no qualms about expressing his support and encouragement by helping the couple to celebrate the religious significance of their marriage by sharing some form of prayer or blessing with them. But he would be wise to make it clear to all concerned that this is not an official Church celebration of their marriage.

What about the clear statement of the Pope in *Familiaris Consortio*?

> The respect due to the sacrament of Matrimony, to the couples themselves and their families, and also to the community of the faithful, forbids any pastor, for whatever reason or pretext even of a pastoral nature, to perform ceremonies of any kind for divorced people who remarry. Such ceremonies would give the impression of the celebration of a new sacramentally valid marriage, and would thus lead people into error concerning the indissolubility of a validly contracted marriage (n. 84).

Does the advice I have given above square with what the Pope is saying? My answer would be 'Yes' and 'No'. 'Yes' in that it squares with the basic concerns that the Pope is trying to safeguard and promote i.e. respect for marriage, for the couple and their families, for the community and for the Church's belief in the indissolubility of marriage. 'No' in that I dissent from the Pope's belief that any kind of ceremony whatsoever would offend against this respect. I suppose the basis for my dissent is in fact the whole approach to marriage, indissolubility and second marriage which I have outlined in this book. If this is interpreted as opposition, at least I think it satisfies the Pope's two criteria by being constructive and in solidarity.

At the level of more general pastoral policy I believe that, in the kind of instance under discussion, the Roman Catholic Church should devise some kind of programme of more positive support for a couple who have made a conscientious decision to enter a second marriage.

The process of change in pastoral practice

It would hardly be a good thing to reverse virtually by accident a pastoral discipline which has held almost uninterrupted possession, at least in the Western Church. But would that be an accurate description of what I am suggesting should happen with regard to the sacraments and those in a second marriage? In other words, would such a change be happening *by accident*? To answer this question we need to consider the relationship between pastoral change and theological development.

Theology, authority and life

It is only to be expected that any major change in theological understanding will automatically result in some kind of change of emphasis in Christian living. This does not need to wait to be mediated through some legal process, as though Christians were expected to sit back and wait for alternative instructions for Christian living to be issued. As a normal rule, it is good that changes in pastoral practice should in the first instance occur naturally as a kind of instinctive reaction to a new way of understanding things. This is a much healthier process than that of having practical changes imposed by edict from on high. If they develop naturally, they have more chance of being able to find their own right level as people learn to discern what is appropriate in particular situations. The adoption of these changes as official policy should occur at a later stage in the process. By then what is pastorally helpful would have been sifted by experience from what is harmful or unnecessary. For a change in pastoral practice to occur informally, therefore, should not be regarded as something harmful to the Church. Nor should it be considered to be occurring by accident, if by that is meant occurring without deep theological reflection and serious pastoral concern. In fact, for change to be able to occur in this informal way can be a very healthy sign that the whole Church is beginning to play a more active part in theological reflection and pastoral discernment.

Obviously, what is very important is the quality of theological reflection which precedes and accompanies such change in pastoral policy. In such an area as the living out of marriage for Christians, there is no doubt that theological reflection cannot be considered adequate if Christian married couples are not given the opportunity to make their full contribution to the discussion. Yet clearly they are not the only ones with something to say in this area. Many others can contribute to the Church's understanding of marriage by their practical experience or their research. Even moral theologians have a role to play, though probably a very modest one, in this discussion!

The fruit of such open discussion in the Church should be teaching which is rich in its content and easily understandable in its presentation. It should also be teaching which makes sense of people's experience, interpreting and challenging it in the light of the Gospel. A number of bishops in the 1980 Synod made a strong plea for teaching of this calibre.

The best and most authoritative teaching document on marriage to come from the Roman Catholic Church in recent years is undoubtedly the Vatican II Pastoral Constitution, *The Church in the Modern World*, nn. 47–52. It was welcomed by all concerned as an extremely good, though necessarily incomplete, expression of what they as Christians really believe about marriage. In a sense, this 'reception' confirms and even increases its authority. The same cannot be said of some more recent statements dealing with specific issues of marriage and sexuality e.g. *Humanae Vitae*, and the *Declaration on Certain Questions of Sexual Ethics*. These have not been 'received' in the same way. Incidentally, one of the main reasons given, especially by theologians, for their critical reception has been the fact that in some respects these documents seem to retreat from rather than develop the teaching of Vatican II. This critical reception lessens the authority of these statements and is an indication of their inadequacy as expressions of what Catholics really believe in this area. This is not reducing Catholic teaching to a head-count or a majority vote; but it is recognizing the essential, though admittedly partial, role played by the Christian common sense of the ordinary faithful. Difficult though this notion is to apply in practice, it is not completely devoid of practical significance. At least one of its immediate implications would seem to be the need to have confidence in the process of open discussion in the Church.

It seems to me that the position put forward in this book, including its practical consequences as outlined in this final chapter, is trying to draw out the implications of the Christian vision of marriage as taught authoritatively by the Second Vatican Council in its Pastoral Constitution, *The Church in the Modern World*. This probably explains why, as far as I can judge, this position is in tune with the deeply-felt convictions of many Christian married couples. The opposite seems to be the case with the position which would refuse the sacraments to the divorced-remarried unless they separate or live as brother and sister. It is not so easy to present that position as flowing from Vatican II's theology of marriage and it seems to go contrary to the pastoral sense of many married Christians.

I would suggest, therefore, that serious theological reflection has prepared the way for such a pastoral development in the Church and this reflection has not been undertaken independently of the teaching authority of the Church. In fact, its starting point has been given authoritative standing in the Church in the teaching of Vatican II. I am not denying that currently there is disagreement about pastoral practice in this question among those who in their different ways exercise teaching authority in the Church. However, what is ironical is that those whose role is to give official articulation to the Church's position sometimes seem committed to positions which are not fully in line with the fundamental teaching of Vatican II; whereas those whose teaching authority is more associated with a combination of experience and theological reflection (i.e. married couples and theologians) favour a view which seems more committed to the teaching of Vatican II. Regardless of how this divergence of view is finally resolved, it is hardly accurate to say that the kind of pastoral development discussed in this chapter would be occurring by accident or without deep theological reflection and concern for the authoritative teaching of the Church.

Change seen in context

In considering whether a change in an ancient practice might not be occurring by accident and so be something to be deplored, the other factor to be borne in mind is that the impact of a particular change can only be assessed by looking at its wider context.

If the new way of understanding of marriage is accepted as the basis for developing pastoral care in the field of marriage, what will be experienced initially by people will be a major redeployment of attention and resources into the area of marriage education, preparation and support. In an age in which divorce can too easily be taken for granted, this should be seen as a radical alternative to a permissive attitude to marriage breakdown. The Church is refusing to go along with any kind of 'divorce mentality'. For her the promotion of the stability of marriage is a prime pastoral priority. Because it will be concentrating so much of its resources into this work, far from overturning its traditional belief, the Church will be giving it a power and an effectiveness which it has never had before. The overall context will be one of a strengthening and a healthy development of its traditional concern for the indissolubility of marriage. In such a context where very positive steps are taken to enable couples to develop at a very personal level in their marriages that indissolubility to which they have pledged themselves, there will be less danger that a milder sacramental policy towards the divorced-remarried will be interpreted as a denial of indissolubility by the Church. It has more chance of being seen for what it really is: the church trying to care for these people with that Gospel-inspired attitude which Pope

John Paul described so beautifully in his closing address to the 1980 Synod: 'The Church . . . must show herself a merciful mother towards them.'

APPENDIX

Life-giving Love and Family Planning*

According to the teaching of Vatican II, the answer which a couple should give to the question 'Why do you not want to have a child at present, or even for the foreseeable future?' should always be: 'Because we want to respect the life-giving character of our married love.' For some this might be why they decide not to have a child in the first few years of their marriage; they want to give themselves sufficient time to grow more alive as a loving couple. However, they would need to realize the great contribution that a child of their own can bring to the growth of their love for each other; and they would also need to face honestly where they are putting their priorities. Their own rich love for each other is far more important for their future family than a well-furnished house and the million other amenities of our consumer society. In their desire to get everything just right before having their first child the couple will need to face honestly the possibility that the growth of their own love for each other might need the shared stimulus of a child of their own long before they are able to set up the model household materially.

For other couples 'Because we want to respect the life-giving character of our married love' might be the reason why they decide not to have any further children. They feel that their responsibilities to each other and to their existing children make it prudent for them not to have any further children. Once again this is a decision made for life-giving reasons. The decision is theirs to make but at times they might be wise to get advice from others. For instance, a couple who are absolutely ideal parents might be helped to realize what a great gift God has given them as a couple. This might lead them to decide to have a larger

* See above, pp. 24–6.

family than is commonly the practice today. Their love might be so rich in life-giving potential that it might be ungenerous not to make a fuller gift of it.

What needs to be made clear, therefore, is that the *intention* not to have a child for the present or for the foreseeable future can be (though not necessarily is) a life-giving decision and so one which is a fully responsible Christian decision. A calm discussion about methods of birth control is impossible unless this teaching of Vatican II which is repeated in *Humanae Vitae* is clearly understood.

When the question of methods of birth control is discussed, it might be helpful to begin by looking at the various methods with the following question in mind: 'How does this method fit in with the life-giving character of a couple's married love, understanding life-giving in the full sense outlined above?' In order to undertake such an evaluation a person would need to have accurate factual knowledge of the various methods and would also need to know about reliability, health hazards etc. To answer the above question one would need to break it down further and ask:

a) 'How does this way of acting affect their love as life-giving to each other?' In other words, does it interfere with the natural flow of their making love together, does it put all the responsibility on either husband or wife, does it subject one partner to great discomfort or even a health hazard or a bodily mutilation, is it a method in which they carry a shared responsibility, is it permanent or can they change their decision later etc?

b) 'How does this way of acting affect their love as life-giving in the sense of giving life to children?' In other words, they would need to see whether a particular method works by way of an abortifacient.

In looking at the various methods from both these angles, the question of a method's reliability must also be looked at. The importance to the couple of the reliability factor will depend on how important it is to them not to have a child at present. For a few it might even be a matter of life or death; or a wife might have such a dread of another pregnancy that an unreliable method would turn sexual intercourse from a language of love into a virtual nightmare of her.

The method of evaluation outlined above flows as a consequence from the understanding of married love put forward by Vatican II. In that sense it is 'determined by objective standards' as is demanded by the Pastoral Constitution, *The Church in the Modern World*, n. 51. The criteria flowing from the different aspects of life-giving love provide these objective standards. As Paragraph 51 goes on to say: 'based on the nature of the human person and his acts, they preserve the full sense of mutual self-giving and human procreation in the context of true love'. Decision-making according to these criteria involves trying to respect life-giving love to the fullest extent that one's personal and social situation allows.

This personalist approach to marriage and married love is also presented very beautifully by Pope Paul in section 9 of *Humanae Vitae*. However, the Pope goes even further and insists in section 11 that 'any use whatever of marriage must retain its natural potential to procreate human life' and in section 14 he spells out what this means in practice. His basic argument in favour of this teaching is that man 'is not the master of the sources of life but rather the minister of the design established by the Creator' (n. 13) and part of this design is the 'inseparable connection . . . between the unitive significance and the procreative significance which are both inherent to the marriage act' (n. 12).

Many Catholics have welcomed this teaching of Pope Paul but many others have found it either unacceptable or not providing a practical solution to their personal problems. To help them in their dilemma many national hierarchies or conferences have issued pastoral guidelines. Basically the guidance given by many of these hierarchies can be summarized as follows:

a) Those who for genuine reasons of conscience cannot accept the Pope's teaching on this precise point should not regard themselves as guilty of sin nor should they be branded by others as disloyal or inferior Catholics.

b) Those who for motives of life-giving love see no practical alternatives but to use some method of birth-control forbidden by the Pope should not regard their decision as sinful provided they are also sensitive to the demands of their life-giving love both in the choice and in the implementation of the method chosen.

The theological competence of these episcopal statements, their integrity, their loyalty to the teaching of the Church and to the Holy Father, cannot be impugned or called into question. All have emphasised their own acceptance of the Encyclical and the obligations on all Catholics to try to do the same.

It might be helpful to give an example of the kind of advice offered with respect to both dilemmas mentioned above.

a) 'It is a fact that a certain number of Catholics, although admittedly subject to the teaching of the encyclical, find it either extremely difficult or even impossible to make their own all elements of this doctrine. In particular, the argumentation and rational foundation of the encyclical which are only briefly indicated, have failed in some cases to win the assent of men of science, or indeed of some men of culture and education who share in the contemporary empirical and scientific mode of thought. We must appreciate the difficulty experienced by contemporary man in understanding and appropriating some of the points of this encyclical and we must make every effort to learn from the insights of Catholic scientists and intellectuals, who are of undoubted loyalty to Christian truth, to the Church and to the authority of the Holy See. Since they are not denying any point of divine and Catholic faith nor rejecting the teaching authority of the Church, these Catholics should not be considered, or consider themselves, shut off from the body of the faithful. But they should remember that their good faith will be dependent on a sincere self-examination to determine the true motives and grounds for such suspension of assent and on continued effort to understand and deepen their knowledge of the teaching of the Church' (Canadian Bishops, 27 September 1968, full text in Horgan, *Humanae Vitae and the Bishops* pp. 76–83).

b) 'Situations will, no doubt arise in which another pregnancy is unacceptable for reasons such as health or difficult domestic conditions, and where a regime of continence would threaten family peace, marital fidelity or the future of the marriage itself. Here, in common with many other hierarchies, we would say that it is best for the parents to decide what in their given circumstances is the best or only practical way of serving the welfare of the whole family. In this conflict of duties, their responsible decision, though falling short of the ideal, will be subjectively defensible since the aim is not the selfish exclusion of pregnancy but the promotion of the common good of the family' (South African Bishops, 4–8 February 1974; full text in *The Tablet*, 23.3.74).